HACKING WITH KALI LINUX

****

THE ULTIMATE GUIDE FOR BEGINNERS TO HACK WITH KALI LINUX. LEARN ABOUT BASICS OF HACKING, CYBERSECURITY, WIRELESS NETWORKS, WINDOWS, AND PENETRATION TESTING.

BY: FRANK SOLOW

© **Copyright 2019; By Frank Solow All Rights Reserved**

This document is geared towards providing exact and reliable information in regards to the topic and issue covered. The publication is sold with the idea that the publisher is not required to render accounting, officially permitted, or otherwise, qualified services. If advice is necessary, legal or professional, a practiced individual in the profession should be ordered.

- From a Declaration of Principles which was accepted and ap-proved equally by a Committee of the American Bar Association and a Committee of Publishers and Associations.

In no way is, it legal to reproduce, duplicate, or transmit any part of this document in either electronic means or in printed format. Recording of this publication is strictly prohibited and any storage of this document is not allowed unless with written permission from the publisher. All rights reserved.

The information provided herein is stated to be truthful and con-sistent, in that any liability, in terms of inattention or otherwise, by any usage or abuse of any policies, processes, or directions contained within is the solitary and utter responsibility of the recipient reader. Under no circumstances will any legal responsibil-ity or blame be held against the publisher for any reparation, damages, or monetary loss due to the information herein, either directly or indirectly.

Respective authors own all copyrights not held by the publisher.

The information herein is offered for informational purposes sole-ly, and is universal as so. The presentation of the information is without contract or any type of guarantee assurance.

The trademarks that are used are without any consent and the publication of the trademark is without permission or backing by the trademark owner. All trademarks and brands within this book are for clarifying purposes only and are the owned by the owners themselves, not affiliated with this document.

ABOUT THIS BOOK

Does the word hacking scare you? Ironically it is hacking but legal hacking that is doing us good. If this is your first book on hacking then surely you will get some potential insight on hacking after reading this. My book gives a simple overview on ethical hackers.

The term ethical hacker came into surface in the late 1970s when the government of United States of America hired groups of experts called 'red teams' to hack its own hardware and software system. Hackers are cyber criminals or online computer criminals that practice illegal hacking. They penetrate into the security system of a computer network to fetch or extract information.

Technology and internet facilitated the birth and growth of network evils like virus, anti-virus, hacking and ethical hacking. Hacking is a practice of modification of a computer hardware and software system. Illegal breaking of a computer system is a criminal offence. Recently a spurt in hacking of computer systems has opened up several courses on ethical hacking.

A 'white hat' hacker is a moral hacker who runs penetration testing and intrusion testing. Ethical hacking is legally hacking a computer system and penetrating into its database. It aims to secure the loopholes and breaches in the cyber-security system of a company. Legal hacking experts are usually Certified Ethical Hackers who are hired to prevent any potential threat to the computer security system or network. Courses for ethical hacking have become widely popular and many are taking it up as a serious profession. Ethical hacking courses have gathered huge responses all over the world.

The moral hacking experts run several programs to secure the network systems of companies.

A moral hacker has legal permission to breach the software system or the database of a company. The company that allows a probe into its security system must give a legal consent to the moral hacking school in writing.

Moral hackers only look into the security issues of the company and aim to secure the breaches in the system.

The school of moral hackers runs vulnerability assessment to mend loopholes in the internal computer network. They also run software security programs as a preventive measure against illegal hacking

Legal hacking experts detect security weakness in a system which facilitates the entry for online cyber criminals. They conduct these tests mainly to check if the hardware and software programs are effective enough to prevent any unauthorized entry.

The moral experts conduct this test by replicating a cyber attack on the network in order to understand how strong it is against any network intrusion.

The vulnerability test must be done on a regular basis or annually. The company must keep a comprehensive record of the findings and checking for further reference in the future.

Table of Contents

ABOUT THIS BOOK 5

INTRODUCTION 13

WHAT IS KALI LINUX 20

BENEFITS OF KALI LINUX 22

HOW TO INSTALL KALI LINUX 23

HOW A PORT SCAN WORKS 27

THE TOOLS OF HACKING 30

    AIRCRACK-NG- CRACKING PASSWORD / WIFI INSTRUMENT 30

    MALTEGO 31

    NIKTO WEBSITE VULNERABILITY SCANNER . 31

    JOHN THE RIPPER- PASSWORD CRACKING TOOL 33

    SN1PER 34

        FEATURES OF SN1PER 34

    WIRESHARK 35

    OWASP ZED 36

PORT SCANNING TECHNIQUES 37

LEARNING CYBER SECURITY 42

SCANNING THE BOX 46

WHAT IS ETHICAL HACKING? 52

ETHICAL HACKING INSTITUTE 59

EXAMPLES OF ETHICAL HACKING 62

NEED FOR ETHICAL HACKING TRAINING...........66

CAREER IN ETHICAL HACKING 70

TRAINING FOR ETHICAL HACKING AND IT SECURITY...73

THE ILLEGALITY OF COMPUTER HACKING 77

WORLD OF WARCRAFT GOLD DUPE HACKS 80

COMPUTER HACKING...83

SIGNS TO KNOW YOUR COMPUTER HAVE BEEN HACKED 86

WHAT TO DO IF YOUR COMPUTER IS HACKED 101

ETHICAL HACKING SALARY..............................105

WIRELESS HACKS...109

THE FEAR OF BEING HACKED AND ATTACKED ON FACEBOOK...116

POINTS TO CONSIDER IN SECURING WEBSITES AND CREATING VIRTUAL KEYWORDS AGAINST HACKING PASSWORDS....................................125

IPHONE HACKS & SOFTWARE 131

SECURING YOUR COMPUTER AND PERSONAL ACCOUNTS FROM HACKING ATTEMPTS 134

REALITY HACKING 138

SECURE WORDPRESS SITES..............................148

BASICS OF ETHICAL HACKING AND
PENETRATION TESTING...................................152

HOW TO PREVENT SOMEONE FROM HACKING
INTO YOUR EMAIL ACCOUNT..........................157

YOUR EMPLOYEES MUST BE AS
KNOWLEDGEABLE IN HACKING MATTERS.....161

RUNESCAPE HACKS 166

BUY A HACK ATTACK PITCHING MACHINE.....169

FACTS ABOUT WEBSITE SECURITY 173

IPHONE HACKS AND THREATS TO PERSONAL
PRIVACY..177

HOW TO REPAIR HACKED BLOG......................181

HOW CAN HOSTING ACCOUNTS BE EASILY
HACKED 185

PENALTIES FOR EMAIL HACKING 188

HOW TO STOP YOUR HOTMAIL EMAIL
ACCOUNT FROM BEING HACKED....................191

INCREASING TRAFFIC TO YOUR WEBSITE BY
GETTING HACKED..194

WAYS YOUR CAR COULD GET HACKED 199

SOLUTION TO HACKED FACEBOOK OR TWITTER ACCOUNT. 203

SUPERB PRODUCTIVITY HACKS THAT EVERYONE SHOULD TRY..208

SECRET SOCIAL MEDIA HACKS YOU WANT TO TRY NOW...215

BACKING UP YOUR SITE AND HOW TO REDUCE THE RISK OF BEING HACKED 222

CONCLUSION..227

INTRODUCTION

There can be no denial that we live in an era of cyber warfare. You can have little doubt that our era is truly digital. However not everyone is connected to the Internet or using smart phones yet. Not many are aware of the term hacking or how hacking is affecting us and how ethical hacking can make our lives better. We are living within a system and a domain that is too dependable on technology.

Hacking is the new power. It has surfaced as one of the major and prominent cyber crimes which need to be countered. Heard of the saying, diamonds can only cut diamonds; similarly hackers can only prevent hacking. Well does that surprise you? The right term is ethical hacking. Ethical hacking training schools have come forward to produce trained professional hackers directly making our lives a lot more secured.

Among all the crimes that are topping the chart, computer hacking is a serious cyber crime. These effects are manifested in a number of ways which are mostly negative.

Effects of Hacking

Corporate Websites or Governmental Websites

Hacking websites of government companies, Software corporate companies can make the site inaccessible.

Penetration into the Security System

The hacker can directly shut down the site without even directly penetrating into the security system of the site.

Generation of False Traffic

Illegal hackers generate false traffic. This method denies service attack and the capacity of the site to deal with requests is exceeded.

Hacking Software

Hacking of software systems through forced or illegal penetration into the database of a company is a growing menace in the cyberspace.

Shutdown of Online Services

Hacking can lead to the theft of identifying information or the shutdown of online services.

Information Hacking

Those who are not the direct victims of hacking can also be affected due to system of information hacking.

As a preventive measure a lot of companies are now seeking services from trained and certified hackers. Only a skilled hacker can fight against another skilled hacker. The ethical hacking institutes are producing effective and trained hackers. They are trained to assess the damage of the site or the software system done by a hacker. Then the security holes in the sites are corrected. The process may take a few weeks to restore the site.

The ethical school of hackers have come up with several hacking courses that train the students on phishing, Google hacking, session hijacking, vulnerability assessment, buffer overflows, spying technologies, hacking database servers, patch management and creating security policies and many more. These hacking courses are in great demand and many are taking up the white hat hacking jobs as a serious profession. Thus, white hat hackers can be considered as life saviors from illegal hacking that has made our online lives perilous.

Stick with Linux Mint: From the first day of migration, it is recommended that you stick with distributions like Linux Mint, Zorin, Linux Lite e.t.c. There are easy to install and use and they have a huge number of online user base. These users are fairly knowledgeable and kind, ask them what problem you are facing and you will have the correct answer within hours if not within minutes! Linux Mint comes with fairly decent software out of the box. This includes libre office (a free & open source office suite), Thunderbird (Email client), Rhythm (Music Player) and Firefox(you can easily install chrome and chromium). As you get to familiar with Linux environment, you might end up experimenting with different distros and DE (Desktop Environment), however, for now, it is a good idea to stick with Linux

Mint and slowly understanding how Linux works.

Immerse Yourself: Best way to set a relationship with Linux is to make it your daily driver. Without any doubt the first few day's rides would be bumpy and strange, so is everything new and beyond one's comfort zone. A distribution like Linux Mint, Zorin & Ubuntu try to make the journey from Windows or Mac into the universe of Linux smooth and magical! Pretty soon I can assure you that you will be wondering why you ever used anything other than Linux!

Don't be scared of the terminal: Distributions like Ubuntu and Linux Mint are made so that you never really have to open the terminal command line if you don't want to. However, getting to know the command line is profoundly encouraged, and it's not nearly as painful as it looks at first. The command line is really better and more productive than the Graphical User

Interface (GUI) in many cases. What takes several clicks, scrolls, keystrokes, and more clicks in the GUI can usually be accomplished with a single terminal command. That's the simplicity!

Make an alliance with Google: With the passing time, you will come across something in Linux that you desire to do, however, aren't sure what method you should follow. This is where Google will become your best buddy! If there's something you can't figure out how to do in Linux, someone other than you has run into that same problem before. The official Ubuntu Wiki and AskUbuntu forums will apparently be controlling your search outcomes. Conveniently, Linux Mint is built on Ubuntu, so whatever solution works in Ubuntu is virtually guaranteed to work in Linux Mint as well.

WHAT IS KALI LINUX

Kali is the latest and best version of the popular Backtrack Linux penetration test distribution. The creators of the Backtrack series have kept Kali in a format very similar to Backtrack, so anyone familiar with the previous Backtrack platform will be comfortable using it.

Kali has been redesigned from the ground up to be the best and richest distribution of hacking / pentest ethics available. Kali can also run on multiple hardware devices, greatly extending the options for penetration testing or repressive computer security systems.

If you come to Kali from a backstage, after a short training period, you will find that everything is very similar alas your comfort level would grow very quickly.

If you don't know Kali, you'll find an easy-to-use security test platform that includes hundreds of useful and powerful tools to test and protect your network systems.

Kali contains over 300 safety testing tools. Many of Backtrack's redundant tools have been removed and the tools interface optimized. Now you can quickly access the most commonly used tools as they appear in one of the ten main security tool menus. You can also find the same tools and a variety of other tools, all clearly classified in the menu system.

BENEFITS OF KALI LINUX

With Kali, you can use similar tools and techniques that a hacker would use to test the security of your network so you can find and solve these problems before a real hacker finds them.

Hackers usually result from a combination of steps when attacking a network. These steps are summarized below:

Enlightenment - Control the destination using multiple sources like collection of information.

Scanning - Planning and examining the network.

Exploitation - The attack of the holes that were found during the scanning process.

Of higher privileges - Increase of an account with less access to the main or system level.

Maintaining Access - Use techniques such as rear doors to provide network access.

Cover their tracks - Deleting logs and editing files in order to hide the intrusion.

An hacker or ethical tester penetration (the good people who have been commissioned to find the gaps before an attacker finds) mimics many of these techniques gradually use the parameters and guidelines that have been set by management to find safety issues.

They then report their findings to management and help solve problems.

HOW TO INSTALL KALI LINUX

As you know, Kali Linux is a famous distribution for hackers, pentesters, forensic and security researchers pre-configured with pre-installed hacking tools that you can use. But Kali is not as easy to use as Ubuntu and Kali's standard environment is not recommended for beginners. So, if you use Ubuntu as your default operating system, you don't need to install Kali Linux as a different distribution. Both Kali Linux and Ubuntu are based on Debian, so you can install all the Kali tools on Ubuntu instead of installing a completely new operating system.

Katoolin

Katoolin (Kali Tools Installer) is a Python script that can install tools that are available in Kali Linux on any Debian distribution. We will try to install it on an Ubuntu machine, but you can use it on any Debian based distribution. It is available on Github. Enter the following to install it.

If your Katoolin is out of date (sometimes) you have to add the key manually for Kali Linux repositories. Now folow the following steps,

- ✓ Start katoolin and add Kali Linux repositories.
- ✓ Then type 1 (ubuntu@ubuntu:~$ sudo katoolin). This option will automatically add Kali's repositories to your "sources.list" file located in "/etc/apt"

directory, so you won't have to do it manually.

✓ Now type 2 to update your system with Kali repositories.

NOTE: It is necessary to remove Kali repositories before running "apt-get upgrade", it can run your system into errors or can cause your Ubuntu Kernel to crash.

✓ Now go back to the main menu using "back" or "gohome" command and then type 2 to view tools categories
✓ You can either browse the categories one by one or you can install all the tools by pressing "0", here we'll install a tools as a quick demo.
✓ It'll take some time to install, after that you can verify "zzuf" installation using "which" command.

Using this "Katoolin" script will automate the process and will make this easier for you. In this way you can install all tools or just some selected tools you want depending upon your requirements. After installing tools, make sure to remove all Kali repositories from your "sources.list" file before upgrading your system. Upgrading Ubuntu with Kali repositories can cause Kernel Panic. If you're using Ubuntu KDE, it is recommended not to install Metasploit Framework because it can cause errors in your Desktop environment. Make sure to read proper documentation to avoid errors.

HOW A PORT SCAN WORKS

With many new security threats arriving everyday, protecting your computer and digital files is even more important. One threat today is port scanning. Port scanning happens to most people whether they realize it or not. Protecting yourself against port scans can help you secure your system from malicious users.

All computers have ports, and services run on these ports. When your computer needs to connect to your mail server in order to check your email, it will open one of these ports and make a connection to download your new email. However sometimes these ports are always on and listening. A port scan occurs when an attacker scans a host to see which ports are open and which are closed or not in use.

Think of a port scan like checking doors and windows of your house to see if it is locked or not. While the attacker may not break into your house he may know that there is a window unlocked and entry can be achieved easily. A port scanner works in much the same way as it checks ports on your computer to see which is closed or open. It is not illegal in most places to do a port scan because basically your just checking if the connection can be made and not actually making a connection to the host. However it is possible to create a Denial of Service attack if port scans are made repeatedly.

Many firewalls can protect you against port scans. A firewall is a program that monitors outgoing and incoming connections to your computer. A firewall may open all ports on your system to effectively stop scans from showing any ports. While this approach works in many cases. Port Scans have advanced with new techniques such as ICMP port unreachable scans, and NULL scans. While its best to try and filter all port scans to your computer, its also important to realize that any ports that are open and listening need to be investigated.

Leaving open ports on your machine can lead to a system compromise causing lost data, and possibly identity theft. A port scan of your own system can show you exactly what an attacker sees and what sort of action you need to take to prevent an attack on your system.

One of the most popular port scanners available today is NMap from insecure.org. NMap is available for free download and is available for UNIX and Windows based systems. Its important to understand how NMap works so you can take the same approach as an attacker would against you. There are other port scanning software available and each has their own port scanning features. However NMap is by far the most popular and is loaded with features and different sorts of port scans you can perform.

While a port scan may not mean your system is about to be attacked. Its important to note that if a port scan occurs, someone knows about a weakness in your system if there is one. This thought alone is enough to consider auditing your firewall for port scan attempts.

THE TOOLS OF HACKING

AIRCRACK-NG- CRACKING PASSWORD / WIFI INSTRUMENT

The Aircrack suite of Wifi (Wireless) hacking tools is legendary as it is used very effectively in the right hands.

Aircrack-ng is a WEP and WPA-PSK 802.11 key cracking tool that can be used to recover keys when sufficient data packets have been acquired (in monitoring mode).

For those who are committed to penetrating and monitoring wireless networks, Aircrack-ng will be your best friend. It is useful to know that Aircrack-ng implements standard FMS attacks and some changes such as KoreK and PTW attacks to increase their attacks. If you are a mediocre hacker, you will be able to decipher WEP in a few minutes and you should be able to decipher WPA / WPA2.

MALTEGO

Maltego is different in that it works in the field of digital forensics. Maltego is a platform designed to provide a complete picture of IT threats to the business or local environment in which a company operates. One of the great things about Maltego that probably makes it so popular (and included in the top ten of Kali Linux) is the unique perspective of offering network-based, resource-based entities that gather information from across the Web, be it Current Configuration Maltego can locate, aggregate and display this data from a vulnerable router on a network or from the current location of employees during their international visits.

NIKTO WEBSITE VULNERABILITY SCANNER

Nikto is another excellent hacking tool that many pentesters like.

It is worth noting that Nickto is sponsored by Netsparker (another hacking tool that we have also listed in our directory). Nikto is an open-source web server scanner (GPL) capable of scanning and detecting web servers for vulnerabilities.

The system scans a database of over 6800 potentially dangerous files / programs when scanning software stacks. Like other scanners, Nikto looks for outdated (unpatched) versions of over 1300 servers and version-specific problems on over 275 servers. It is interesting to note that Nikto can also check server configuration items, such as: For example, the presence of multiple index files, HTTP server options and the platform will also attempt to identify web servers and installed web applications. Nikto is picked up by any reasonably decent IDS instrument, so it is very useful to perform a pentest white hat / white box.

JOHN THE RIPPER- PASSWORD CRACKING TOOL

It is often displayed as a shortened "JTR". This is an excellent hacking software that can break very complicated passwords.

John the Ripper, usually referred to simply as "John", is a popular password cracking tool most commonly used to perform dictionary attacks. John the ripper takes examples of text strings (from a text file called "word list" that contains popular and complex words found in a real dictionary or password that have been previously violated) and encrypts them on the same Like the cracked password (including both the encryption algorithm and the key) and comparing the output with the encrypted string. This tool can also be used to make various changes to dictionary attacks. Honestly, this is the most helpful tool out there: John the Ripper. If you're a bit confused between John the Ripper and THC Hydra, think of John the Ripper as an offline password cracker, while THC Hydra is an online cracker. Simple.

SN1PER

FEATURES OF SN1PER

• Sn1per is an ideal vulnerability scanner for penetration tests when looking for vulnerabilities.

• It is easy to work with, and it is always up to date.

• The team behind the software, which can be easily uploaded to Kali Linux, has a free plan (community version) and a payment plan.

• The tool is particularly useful for listing and searching for known vulnerabilities.

• If you are learning for OSCP (which requires a lot of enumeration), we recommend that you become familiar with Sn1per.

We recommend using this tool together with Metasploit or Nessus. So, if you get the same result, you surely know that you care about something.

WIRESHARK

Wireshark is a very popular pentesting tool. It is difficult to classify Wireshark into a specific category, but in most cases, it is used to monitor traffic.

Wireshark acquires data packets in a real-time network, then displays them in a human-readable format (in detail). The tool (platform) has been advanced and includes filters, color codes and other features that allow the user to penetrate deeply into network traffic and to control individual packets. If you want to become a penetration tester or work as a computer security expert, you need to learn how to use Wireshark.

There are countless resources to learn about Wireshark and of particular interest is the Wireshark certification, which you can access and add to your LinkedIn profile.

OWASP ZED

Zed Attack Proxy (ZAP) is one of the most popular OWASP projects today. It is very likely that you are familiar with OWASP, not least the OWASP list of the ten most common threats that drive Web application security. This software piracy and pentesting tool is both very efficient and easy to use and finds vulnerabilities in web applications. ZAP is a popular tool as it provides a lot of support and the OWASP community is an excellent resource for those working with computer security. ZAP offers automatic scanners and various tools that allow you, like cyber pro, to manually detect vulnerabilities. Understanding and mastering this tool would also be useful for your career as a penetration tester. If you are a developer, you should definitely learn how to handle this "hacking tool" very well.

PORT SCANNING TECHNIQUES

SecurityWeek Network reported "The simple truth is that the only way to be sure that we actually analyze all network malware-related traffic is to perform a full inspection of all traffic on all ports." One of the primary tools used by malicious attackers to assess your network weaknesses is the port scan. By running a port scan an attacker can find out what "doors" into your network are open. Once they know that information they can begin to research what sorts of vulnerabilities or exploits that might open up to a network. It is vital that organizations restrict and control the traffic that is allowed into the network. One of the important attacks that Snort NIDS detects is port scanning.

The Secret Knock Can Open Your System," port scanning is similar to a thief going through your neighborhood and checking every door and window on each house to see which are open and which are locked. TCP (Transmission

Control Protocol) and UDP (User Datagram Protocol) are two of the protocols that make up the TCP/IP protocol suite which is used universally to communicate on the Internet. Each of these has ports 0 through 65535 available, so essentially there are more than 65,000 doors to lock.

The first 1024 TCP ports are called the Well-Known Ports and are associated with standard services such as FTP, HTTP, SMTP, or DNS. Some of the addresses over 1023 also have commonly associated services, but the majority of these ports are not associated with any service and are available for a program or application to use to communicate.

TCP scanning is the most common type of scanning which uses the operating system's network functions. The attacker sends a SYN packet to the victim and in case the port is open then an ACK packet is sent back to the attacker by the victim thus notifying that the port is open. This process is termed as 3-way handshaking.

UDP Scanning is a connectionless protocol. This means that there is no notification sent back to the attacker whether the packet has been received or dropped by the victim's network. If a UDP packet is sent to a port that is not open, the system will respond with an ICMP port unreachable message. Most UDP port scanners use this scanning method and use the absence of a response to infer that a port is open.

What is Stealth TCP Port Scanning?

If the port scan is being done with malicious intent, the intruder would generally prefer to go undetected. Network security applications such as Network Intrusion Detection Systems (NIDS) can be configured to alert administrators if they detect connection requests across a broad range of ports from a single host. To get around this the intruder can do the port scan in strobe or stealth mode. Strobing limits the ports to a smaller target set rather than blanket scanning all 65536 ports. Stealth scanning uses techniques such as slowing the scan. By scanning the ports over a much longer period of time you reduce the chance that the target will trigger an alert."

Network intrusion detection systems (NIDS) monitors packets on the network wire and attempts to discover an intruder by matching the attack pattern to a database of known attack patterns. A typical example is looking for a large number of TCP connection requests (SYN) to many different ports on a target machine, thus discovering if someone is attempting a TCP port scan. A network intrusion detection system sniffs network traffic by promiscuously watching all network traffic."

Snort is an open source network intrusion detection system, capable of performing real-time traffic analysis and packet logging on IP networks. It can perform protocol analysis, content searching/matching, and can be used to detect a variety of attacks and probes, such as buffer overflows, stealth port scans, CGI attacks, SMB probes, OS fingerprinting attempts, and much more.

LEARNING CYBER SECURITY

Computers have come to be an essential part of our life today. This requires IT professionals to have a good understanding of IT security foundations. These security foundations require an understanding of the controls needed to protect the confidentiality, integrity, and availability of the information.

Without strong controls cyber hackers and cyber criminals can threaten systems, expose information, and potentially halt operations. These types of attacks can create serious business losses. Cyber criminals and cyber hackers can target firewalls, IDS, and access control to enter the network and thereby causing serious damage. The problem of cyber crime gives rise to the need for cyber security training and aggressive controls to protect data. Anyone considering learning cyber foundations can learn the proper handling methods of sensitive corporate data.

The purpose of such training is to address aspects such as IT security and protection, responsibilities of people handling information, availability of data confidentiality, and how to handle problems such as unauthorized data modification, disruption, destruction and misuse of information.

Any cyber security foundations training must cover aspects such as Network Security and Administration, Secure Software Development, Computer Forensics and Penetration Testing. Here is a look at what such training should cover as a minimum:

• Standard IT security terminology

• Techniques that provide hands-on experience with mitigating controls. This means you must learn real skills to handling breaches in security.

• Current and future cyber security roles and positions that will be required by businesses to successfully design secure IT computer networks

• Aspects and concerns such as the hacker attack cycle and 7 steps of cyber attacks

• Technical aspects of handling security breach should be addressed comprehensively, so that you are intend in-depth knowledge on how to prevent security breaches

• The basic aspects of security zones so that you are aware of defense in depth

• Auditing requirements.

With the internet bridging distances and making the whole world a global marketplace, computers have come to be only more important. There are several companies that offer online courses that cater to all the requirements related to computer security that an individual might have. Registering for a course that takes care of all your requirements is important. The course must be such that equips you the power to take on the challenges of the present day competitive world. With knowledge by your side and the confidence to take on the world, success is sure to be yours.

SCANNING THE BOX

This chapter provides details on the scanning phase of any penetration test (blackbox, whitebox, gray box). Let's start from defining the types of scan we can use while performing a penetration test.

Scanning the box means performing the scan on the target to blueprint its security measures and than to penetrate into the box.

Types of scan we can perform on the selected target:

1. OS Scan (OS fingerprinting)

2. Port Scan (Service detection)

3. Vulnerability scan (finding the hole)

Let's discuss the above types in detail:

OS Scan (OS fingerprinting):

When we are performing a pen-test we need to detect what OS is being running on the remote machine so what we can search for its related critical patches and vulnerabilities. OS fingerprinting is also known as banner grabbing.Banner grabbing and operating system identification - can also be defined as fingerprinting the TCP/IP stack. Banner grabbing is the process of opening a connection and reading the banner or response sent by the application

Following are the two techniques used to detect OS fingerprint:

a. Active Stack fingerprinting

b. Passive Stack fingerprinting

Active stack fingerprinting:

Active stack fingerprinting is the most common form of fingerprinting. It involves sending data to a system to see how the system responds. It's based on the fact that various operating system vendors implement the TCP stack differently, and responses will differ based on the operating system. The responses are then compared to a database to determine the operating system. Active stack fingerprinting is detectable because it repeatedly attempts to connect with the same target system.

Passive stack fingerprinting:

Passive stack fingerprinting is stealthier and involves examining traffic on the network to determine the operating system. It uses sniffing techniques instead of scanning techniques. Passive stack fingerprinting usually goes undetected by an IDS or other security system but is less accurate than active fingerprinting.

Port Scan (Service detection):

Port scanning is used to gather information about a test target from a remote network location. Specifically, port scanners attempt to locate which network services are available for connection on each target host by probing each of the designated (or default) network ports or services on the target system.

In a broad approach Port scanning is the process of identifying open and available TCP/IP ports on a system. Port-scanning tools enable a hacker to learn about the services available on a given system. Each service or application on a machine is associated with a well-known port number. For example, a port-scanning tool that identifies port 80 as open indicates a web server is running on that system. Hackers need to be familiar with well-known port numbers.

Vulnerability scanning (finding the hole):

The primary distinction between a port scan and a vulnerability scan is that vulnerability scan attempt to exercise (known) vulnerabilities on their targeted systems, whereas port scan only produce an inventory of available services. That said the distinguishing factors between port and vulnerability scan are often times blurred.It is the automated process of proactively identifying vulnerabilities of computing systems in a network in order to determine if and where a system can be exploited and/or threatened. While public servers are important for communication and data transfer over the Internet, they open the door to potential security breaches by threat agents, such as malicious hackers. Vulnerability scanning employs software that seeks out security flaws based on a database of known flaws, testing systems for the occurrence of these flaws and generating a report of the findings that an individual or an enterprise can use to tighten the network's security. Vulnerability scanning typically refers to the scanning of systems that are connected to the Internet but can also refer to system audits on internal networks that are not connected to the Internet in order to assess the threat of rogue software or malicious employees in an enterprise.

Tools available for Scanning the BOX

Port Scanners: de-factor for port scanning is NMAP some more tools are available for port scanning are net cat, advance port scanner, super scan etc

Vulnerability scanners: de-facto standard for vulnerability scanning is Nessus some more tools are available for vulnerability scanning are GFI Languard, SARA, Shadow security scanner etc.

WHAT IS ETHICAL HACKING?

Ethical Hacking is an inalienable part of the cybersecurity. The vast ever-increasing business activities of the organizations due to globalization raise security concerns to a large extent which if ignored may cause a huge loss in terms of a breach in the system hence data theft. Every prospering organization knows very well the importance of securing information. Certified ethical hackers thus bear great importance in this whole scenario.

We all know and have heard of hacking which is notorious in its nature. The malicious hackers breach the systems and exploit it. The same thing Ethical Hackers do but in a legitimate and lawful way for a constructive purpose where they search for vulnerabilities in the system and protect it from the potential attacks and threats. Ethical hackers ensure safety of information, help organizations by improving the system security

Why organizations need ethical hackers

There are persistent cyber-attacks that caused huge data loss and incurred great expenses' aftermath to recover it. It was the EC-Council, a leading IT Organization in Cyber-security certification programs, for the very first time brought the concept of Ethical hacking in the wake of the terrorist attack of September 11. By now though with mixed responses, Ethical hacking has been accepted in the IT world for its greater utility in securing systems and network. Ethical hackers think the very way the malicious hacker does and stop unlawful activities by identifying threats and vulnerabilities.

Need of security professionals or better say certified ethical hackers is felt than ever before. Cyber threats keep ethical hackers on toes to protect the network and system effectively. No company can afford confidential data loss. Though the concept of Ethical hacking has come recently on the horizons, security concerns were already in place and the organizations merely were in the work of patching up. But now it has created urgency to control the breaches owing to the ever-increasing business of the organizations.

Ethical hackers, in this whole affair, can be a savior for the businesses. Ethical hackers help organizations in following way -

Safeguard systems thereby protect information from the attacks by building a foolproof computer system which prevents illegal access

Ethical hackers manage Preventive measures to avoid hacking threats

Create security awareness

Regular network testing for efficient defense periodically

Importance of CEH Certification Programme

Experience matters but the systematic knowledge of the tools and techniques is needed for the purpose. Certification programme - CEH-Certified Ethical Hacker makes you updated in the modern technology of the subject field. Ethical hacking, for instance, is the area of work where you must keep yourself updated with new technology, tools, and techniques. Malicious hackers devise new ways to breach and exploit the system thus you must be a step ahead of them, you must, as an ethical hacker, take preventive actions and protect the organization's network and computer system. Getting training through an Ethical hacking certification programme helps you validate your skills and improve knowledge.

Nature of CEH certification programme

Exam Code: 312-50 (ECC Exam), 312 (VUE)

Who can appear for CEH certification: An IT professional with 2 years of experience in the field of information security is eligible for the course.

Exam Nature: A 4 hours long test will be conducted online. Multiple choice format question paper would contain 125 questions.

Delivery of Test: ECC Exam, VUE

Exam Cost: $100 Non-refundable Application Fee. $950 Exam Voucher.

Choosing the best IT training institute

No doubt the course is worth pursuing for greater returns in terms of career growth and remuneration for the related job profile, but choosing a right training institute bears huge importance. A quality training institute offers a great learning environment, dedicated team of trainers. You should be very apt in your decision of joining the training center for CEH Certification programme by EC-Council.

There are such a few recommended institutions in India that provide CEH certification training and SSDN Education tops the list. You can join SSDN Education for CEH Certification training without any doubts.

SSDN Education, a brand name in IT training world, has been persistently generating qualified workforce for the corporate world. SSDN Education has been in IT and process management training arena for years and considered a leading CEH training institute in Gurgaon and NCR. Ethical hacking training is being delivered by the highly qualified CEH trainers at

SSDN. The trail of success rate depicts the worthiness of SSDN. Well-equipped labs provide the highest level of the learning experience. No matter you are just a beginner or mid-career professional, SSDN makes you enough confident and competent that you start thinking like an entrepreneur and an accomplished IT professional.

ETHICAL HACKING INSTITUTE

Are you new to Linux or thinking of using it for the first time? Hold on! What the heck I'm saying here! There's no word called " New to Linux" or " first time Linux user". Without your conscious, you probably use it every single day! And you were thinking Linux meant for the programming nerds, hackers and going through Linux means using that good old green terminal!

That's racist you know!!

The main question should be- are you new to personal Linux computing? Well if your answer is "Yes", then worry not, a superior operating system is ready to be served for his only master. See what I did there? If not, I mean to say that you and only YOU are the owners of your hardware and software. No one going to install some crappy app that you don't need or change the system setting while you are enjoying good old " funny kitty video" on the internet!

In the world of Linux personal computing, there is a plethora of choice to choose from. People from Linux planet call this "Distributions". What this means is, while the primary system 'Kernel" is identical, the look & feel and the entire ecosystem can be different.

Here are some others you may have heard of:

Fedora

Zorin

openSUSE

Debian

Those are the biggest distribution in terms of users. However, as a beginner, you should use " Linux Mint cinnamon edition". It closely resembles your windows PC and if you are coming from the world of fruit, I will suggest giving a try to the "Elementary OS" or "Deepin OS". They closely resemble the Mac ecosystem.

EXAMPLES OF ETHICAL HACKING

It's funny, because the concept of carrying out what is basically a malicious attack ethically has certainly evolved people's understanding on the subject of hacking. People tend to immediately associate this with negative actions and intentions, because they only know the negative effects. In short, most will believe there can be little or no positive application for it, but of course that is just not true.

When used for good, it's good!

When used as a means to improve an individual or a company's online defences, we find this "malicious act" rather beneficial. The practice of breaking into, or bypassing an online system or network in order to expose its flaws for further improvement is entirely ethical (and you can make a nice living doing it too.)

Examples of ethical hacking include exploiting or exposing a website in order to discover its weak points. Then report your findings and let the appropriate person fix those vulnerabilities. Then in the future, should they come under attack, they will be that bit safer. You are actually preparing them for any real threat of attack because you are eliminating the areas which could possibly be exploited against them.

There are a lot of examples of ethical hacking, including one which happened in the early days of computers. Back then, the United States Air Force used it to conduct a security evaluation of an operating system. In doing so, they were able to discover flaws like vulnerable hardware, software, and procedural security. They determined that even with a relatively low level of effort, their security can be bypassed and the intruder would get away with precious information. Thanks to ethical hacking, they were able to stop such an incident from happening. The people who carried out this task treated the situation as if they really were the enemy, doing all they could to break into the system. This way, they could determine exactly how secure their system was. This is perhaps one of the best examples of ethical hacking because they were sanctioned by the people who were responsible for the creation of the said online system. They recognized the need for such action because they know that there are a lot of people capable of doing the same thing, or inflicting the same harm to their system.

From all the examples of ethical hacking, perhaps you can clearly relate to the practices of known Operating Systems being used today. Makers of these Operating Systems perform their own ethical hacks to their systems before actually launching their products to the public. This is to prevent possible attacks that could be perpetrated by hackers. This is somehow a means of quality control during the system's development phase, to make sure that all the weaknesses of their Operating Systems are covered, since it will be marketed for public use.

Ethical hacking is a very useful approach in defending your precious online systems. By tapping into the abilities and potential of white hat hackers, you are able to take on and prevent damages caused by the real hackers.

NEED FOR ETHICAL HACKING TRAINING

Running a business or personal pursuit online these days is not without ingrained challenges. People have now started entering other sites and accounts in order to tamper with vital information and also to sneak in and collect data. This form of sneaking in is termed as 'hacking' and this needs to be stopped! In order to prevent people from entering your account, it needs to be checked regularly. This is the work of an ethical hacker. This is why there is an increase in the need for ethical hacking training the world over today.

Who is an ethical hacker?

In computer terminology, people with different intentions who enter accounts of others are identified as people wearing different colored hats! In this regard, the ethical hacker is a person who wears a white hat. The main function of a person with hacker training is to enter or penetrate into a system to check for the security and the protection of the ingrained IT system. These white hackers are experts in the field of computer security and they are trained to penetrate the systems of a company or individuals that contain all vital and highly sensitive information. It is important to note that such systems on the outside seem supposedly very secure but remain exposed to threats from fraudulent approach.

In order to be trained for this activity the candidates undergo ethical hacking training. Companies employ either one of them or a group in order to check for the reliability of the system. When they work as a team they are called red or tiger teams. Through ethical hacker training they gain knowledge about the different ways in which it is possible to hack into a system and they use the methods to sneak in and check for loop holes. There are many organizations that now offer certified ethical hacker training programs.

What is the significance of ethical hacker training?

Many companies are not yet convinced about the need for checking into the systems with the help of ethical hacking. They are of the opinion that no one would hack into their system. The ignorance could cost the company millions of dollars. However, if the system is not checked by an expert and the information gets hacked by wrong people, very important and crucial information can leak out into the hands of the wrong people. Therefore it is very important to either employ an expert who has completed certified ethical hacker training or give in-house employees hacker training. These people help to find and plug the problems within the system and protect data from fraudulent use.

When left exposed to hackers, these fraudulent people also hack into files of the employees and upload viruses into a system that could shut down and corrupt the entire network. The after-effects of such kind of hacking could result in the loss of important and classified information. This could cost the company many of its clients, who would stop trusting the company with important information. These are some of the reasons why employing people who have undergone ethical hacking training becomes extremely important for the well being of the company and the well being of the employees. After all, your IT health is in your hands!

CAREER IN ETHICAL HACKING

Ethical hacking is the process of penetrating or intruding in a computer system for the purpose of security testing. Hackers who conduct ethical hacking are hired by companies to conduct penetration testing. These hackers are experts in computer security, as they play a crucial part in ensuring a company's IT system security. If you want to pursue a career in ethical hacking, you have to be knowledgeable in social engineering techniques and you must be able to properly identify the weaknesses and vulnerabilities of IT systems so that necessary measures may be taken to properly secure them.

Ethical hackers must explore different hacking methods to check if a company's IT system can be penetrated using any of these methods. Their job is basically to mimic the actions of a hacker and exhaust all possible hacking options to prevent illegal hacking. Pursuing a career in ethical hacking can be a very rewarding and profitable venture, as ethical hackers are usually paid a lot. However, before you can become an ethical hacker, you need to have adequate experience and knowledge in networking and programming. You should also have a good grasp of all available operating systems so that you can properly anticipate hacking methods.

If you want to become a licensed ethical hacker, then a course that is related to cyber security and IT is a prerequisite. You should also be knowledgeable about both the software and hardware involved in illegal hacking. Hacking is a serious Internet crime that can be done by anyone who has enough knowledge about how to penetrate a computer system. This knowledge is often always abused to get access to confidential information such as personal information, financial information and other such confidentialities. Illegal hacking is oftentimes used as a tool for theft.

Increasing security measures have to be employed to protect computer systems from this heinous crime. A career in ethical hacking is highly profitable because there is an increasing demand for ethical hackers.

Since ethical hacking takes a lot of skill, necessary training is important before you can become licensed as an ethical hacker. You will also have to be trained in the ethical aspect of hacking. As a hacker, you will be able to enter confidential systems that contain hundreds of vital information. Before you can pursue a career in ethical hacking, you will have to be briefed when it comes to the ethical aspect of the business. It takes a certain degree of trust before you can be hired as an ethical hacker so aside from having all the necessary skills, you will also need to earn this trust.

TRAINING FOR ETHICAL HACKING AND IT SECURITY

In the emerging IT sector, a very hot trend is to become an ethical hacker or an IT security expert. An ethical hacker is none other than a penetration testing expert who is basically employed by an organization for fixing the whole organization system against any outside vulnerable attacks like hacking, loss of data etc. For becoming a certified ethical hacker, one has to clear the certification exams after going through a professional ethical hacking training conducted by various countries worldwide. For this, a professional ethical hacking training is required in which a candidate is taught about the A to Z penetration testing mechanism. The main focus under this training is to educate the candidate about all the pros and cons of conducting and leading a "pen test" including the important business documents needed to and after the testing. Ethical Hacking Training is available in all over the world and is very famous among Design and Development (DAD) community.

Ethical Hackers are needed for many important reasons as follows:-

- Internet Security companies requires certified ethical hacking experts who can hack their systems in order to make ensure that the current security system of those companies is secured on a strong basis.

- Criminal Forensic Labs and Law enforcement Agencies also requires ethical hacking experts who are having relevant experience in gathering information for important evidence purposes.

In relevancy to ethical hacking, Information security training is also an important factor which involves protection of information system from unauthorized access or any other vulnerable alteration. For this purpose, IT security training is also required for those computer professionals who are directly associated with the data security of the company.

IT security consists of three important quality attributes as follows:-

- Conceptual Data Integrity which includes the information about the design of modules or components as well as factors such as coding style and variable naming.

- Confidentiality which is used to ensure that information of an organization is shared only among authorized persons.

- Availability which ensures that the processing information is accessible on a 24 * 7 hours basis.

IT Security Training is very helpful in making and organization's security program to run effectively. It also increases the awareness about data security among the employees. So an IT firm must provide professional ethical hacking training and IT security training to all its employees from time to time.

Nowadays, the IT people who have the certification in IT Security have a good exposure in IT industry for their bright future. They can shape their career in own way and have a secure career. Most of the people start their career with security training. There is a boom in IT industry to save and transact the data in a secure manner that is the main reason behind for the evolution of IT Security in IT Industry.

THE ILLEGALITY OF COMPUTER HACKING

When the Internet became a part of daily life in the late 1990s, there was an influx in computer hacking because it became a big source of personal information. Computer hacking, regardless of the hacker's intent, is highly illegal and may be punishable by fines and jail time.

There are many reasons why people hack into computers. Some do it for the fun, while others do it to steal information and money. Even if an individual does not intend to steal another person's identity or money, the act of hacking itself is illegal, and he or she may be charged accordingly.

Though individuals have become more mindful of computer hacking's prevalence, it still happens with great frequency. An individual may hack a private person's computer or a corporate mainframe to gain information access. These actions are both illegal.

Hacking may take many forms, including:

Planting viruses

Stealing information

Exploiting security systems

Cracking passwords

Impersonating another person

Each of these actions may land an individual in jail. Though this is considered a white collar crime, it is still a serious criminal offense that may damage an individual's reputation in addition to causing him or her to serve time in prison and pay fines.

Individuals who have been accused of committing a crime of computer hacking should know their legal rights. Every individual who faces criminal charges is entitled to a defense lawyer. Having the right defense lawyer can sometimes make all the difference in a case.

It is important for individuals accused of computer hacking to have a defense team that understands the crime and is able to defend the charges with a high level of expertise.

If you or someone you love has been accused of computer hacking, discuss your legal rights and options with the criminal defense attorneys at the Inglis Law Office today.

WORLD OF WARCRAFT GOLD DUPE HACKS

If you've been playing World of Warcraft for awhile, then you've probably come across mention of the infamous Gold Dupe Hack, which, it is claimed, will double the WoW gold you have. Well, I've been looking long and hard and just like a bunch of other WoW hacks that are fakes, I've concluded that a legitimate Gold dupe hack for World of Warcraft doesn't exist either.

It appears that one may have existed at one point a couple of years ago (though the evidence is iffy at best), but Blizzard has patched any holes in their gaming software that would have allowed for that kind of exploit anyway, so if it really did exist, it certainly doesn't work anymore . So anyone offering to send you a gold dupe hack is, in all likelihood, actually sending you a keylogger.

A keylogger is basically a trojan or virus that captures the information you are keying and transmits it to someone else. This is how World of Warcraft scammers steal accounts and gold from WoW Players. The easiest players to dupe and steal from are greedy ones. So when you think about it, the gold dupe hack is perfectly named -- because the Dupe is the player who downloads one. Be careful to avoid downloading any so-called "WoW hacks" on torrent networks. I can just about guarantee that you'll be downloading a virus of some kind rather than the mythical script that you are hoping to find.

There are easier ways of getting more gold into your account. There are several different WoW gold guides available that explain all the shortcuts and the best strategies to use to get gold faster and none of them involved cheating, hacks or bots of any kind. My preferred guide is Derek's Gold Guide, so I would take a look at that one if you are looking to amass gold in your account. It's a lot cheaper than having your account stolen!

The time you spend fruitlessly searching for a real gold hack could be spent instead using some of the strategies to quickly amass your own gold legitimately without the threat of being banned by Blizzard or having someone else break into your account.

COMPUTER HACKING

Computer hacking is defined as any act of accessing a computer or computer network without the owner's permission. In some cases, hacking requires breaching firewalls or password protections to gain access. In other cases, an individual may hack into a computer that has few or no defenses. Even if there are no defenses to "break" through, simply gaining access to a computer and its information qualifies as criminal computer hacking.

The Intent to Hack

To be convicted of computer hacking, it must be proven that the defendant knowingly gained access to a computer with the intent of breaching without permission. Sometimes individuals, particularly young computer-savvy teenagers, break in to a computer or network just to prove that they can. They may brag about their accomplishment afterward, using the stunt to flaunt their computer abilities. Even though there may not have been an intent to steal or defraud from the hacked system, the defendant can still be criminally charged.

Criminal Charges

When an individual is arrested in Florida for hacking, he or she will be charged with a felony. If the defendant accessed a computer system without authorization but did not intend to steal or defraud, he or she will be charged with a third degree felony. If, however, the hacker broke into the system and planned to defraud the owner of money or information, he or she will be charged with a second degree felony. Past computer hacking offenses have included attempts to steal credit card information, social security numbers, or sensitive company or government information.

Penalties for Hacking

Computer hacking is considered a major threat to company integrity, government confidentiality, and personal security. It is therefore prosecuted aggressively in a court of law. Under Florida law, a third degree felony for hacking can result in a maximum 5 year prison sentence and up to $5,000 in fines. For a hacking offense that involves theft or fraudulent activity, the defendant could be penalized with up to 15 years in prison and a $10,000 fine.

Beyond the immediate court ordered penalties, a hacking offense can destroy an individual's personal and professional reputation. He or she may experience trouble applying to colleges, obtaining scholarships, finding a job, or obtaining a loan. Even many years after your conviction, you could still be negatively affected by your felony computer hacking charge.

SIGNS TO KNOW YOUR COMPUTER HAVE BEEN HACKED

There are several ways in which antivirus scanners try to detect malware. Signature-based detection is the most common method.

This involves searching the contents of a computer's programs for patterns of code that match known viruses. The anti-virus software does this by checking codes against tables that contain the characteristics of known viruses. These tables are called dictionaries of virus signatures.

Because thousands of new viruses are being created every day, the tables of virus signatures have to be updated constantly if the anti-virus software is to be effective. But even if the software is being updated daily, it usually fails to recognise new threats that are less than 24 hours old.

To overcome this limitation and find malware that has not yet been recognised, anti-virus software monitors the behaviour of programs, looking for abnormal behaviour. This technique is called heuristics. The software may also use system monitoring, network traffic detection and virtualized environments to improve their chances of finding new viruses.

Nevertheless, anti-virus software is never 100 percent successful and every day new malware infects computers throughout the world.

Getting hacked

There are three main ways you can get infected with malware.

These are:

(a) running unpatched software, ie software that you have failed to update;

(b) falling for a desirable freebee and downloading a Trojan horse along with the freebee; and

(c) responding to fake phishing emails.

If you can manage to avoid these three failings, you won't have to rely so much on your anti-virus software.

Expecting that some day someone will release anti-virus software that can detect all viruses and other malware with complete accuracy is a vain hope. The best you can do is to keep your security up to date, avoid the three main ways you can get infected, and learn to recognise the signs that suggest your computer has been hacked so that you can take appropriate action.

Here are some sure signs you've been hacked and what you can do about it.

[1] Fake antivirus messages

A fake virus warning message popping up on screen is a pretty sure sign that your computer has been hacked-provided you know it's fake. (To be able to recognise a fake warning, you need to know what a genuine virus warning from your anti-virus software looks like.) The warning will reassure you by saying that it is can scan your system to detect the malware.

Clicking no or cancel to stop the scan won't help, because you computer has already been compromised. The purpose of the fake virus warning (which will always find lots of viruses that need to be eliminated) is to lure you into buying their virus removal service or other product.

Once you click on the link provided for that purpose, you will likely land on a very professional-looking website. There you'll be invited to buy and download the product by filling in your credit card details.

Bingo! As well as having complete control of your system, the hacker now has your personal financial information.

What to do: as soon as you see the fake virus warning message, turn off your computer. Reboot it in safe mode (no networking) and try to uninstall the newly installed software (which can often be uninstalled just like a regular program).

Then, whether you succeed in uninstalling the rogue program or not, restore your system to the state it was in before you got hacked. In the old days, this meant formatting the computer and reinstalling the operating system as well as all programs and data. Nowadays, you can normally revert to a previous state with just a few clicks.

Once you have turned back the clock, so as to speak, restart your computer in the normal way and make sure that the fake virus warning has gone. Then do a complete anti-virus scan to eliminate any traces of the malware.

[2] Unwanted browser toolbars

Finding your browser has a new toolbar is probably the second most common sign of being hacked. Unless you recognize the toolbar, and know that you knowingly downloaded it, you should dump it.

Very often these toolbars come bundled with other software you download. Before you begin a download, you should always read the licensing agreement which may contain a clause allowing other software to be downloaded with the software you want. Hackers know that people seldom read these agreements yet having these kinds of clauses makes the downloading quite legitimate.

What to do: Most browsers allow you to remove toolbars. Check all your toolbars and if you have any doubts about a toolbar, remove it. If you can't find the bogus toolbar in the toolbar list, check to see if your browser has an option to reset it back to its default settings.

If this doesn't work, restore your system to the state it was in before you noticed the new toolbar as described in the previous section.

You can usually avoid malicious toolbars by making sure that all your software is fully up-to-date and by being ultra-cautious when you are offered free software for downloading.

[3] Passwords changed inexplicably

If you discover that a password you use online has been changed without your knowledge then it is highly likely you have been hacked. If not, your internet service provider (ISP) has been compromised.

If you have been hacked, it is probably because you replied with your log-in details to a phishing email that seemed to come from the service for which the password has been changed. If so, the hacker used the information you gave him to log-in and change the password. Now he can avail of the service you were getting or, if it was your internet banking details you sent, steal your money.

What to do: report the change in your password to the online service provider who should be able to get your account back under control within a few minutes. If the log-in information you sent is used on other websites, you should immediately change those passwords also.

Above all, you need to amend your behaviour for the future. Reputable websites will never ask for you log-in details by email. If they do appear to do so, do not click on the link in the email. Instead go directly to the website and log on using your usual method. You should also report the phishing email to the service by telephone or email.

[4] Unexpectedly finding newly installed software

If you find new software in your computer that you don't remember installing, you can be fairly sure that your system has been hacked.

Most malware programs nowadays are trojans and worms which install themselves like legitimate programs, usually as part of a bundle with other programs that you download and install. To avoid this you need to read the licence agreement of the software that you do want to install closely to see if it comes with 'additional' software.

Sometimes you can opt out of these 'free' extras. If you can't, your only option, if you want to be sure you are not going to be hacked, is not to download the software you do want to install.

What to do: the first thing you should do (in Windows) is to go to Add or Remove Programs in the Control Panel. However, the software program may not show up there in the list. In so, there are plenty of programs available on the Internet (usually for free) which will show all the programs installed on your computer and enable you to disable them selectively.

This approach has two problems. Firstly, these free programs cannot guarantee to find every installed program. Secondly, unless you are an expert, you will find it hard to determine what are and what are not legitimate programs.

You could, of course, just disable a program you don't recognise and restart your computer. If some functionality you need is no longer working, you can re-enable the program.

However, your best bet in my view is to stop taking risks (and wasting time) by calling an expert technician at an online computer maintenance company who can scrutinise your system for illegitimate programs and delete them as necessary.

[5] Cursor moving around and starting programs

Cursors can move around randomly at times without doing anything in particular. This is usually due to problems with hardware.

But if your cursor begins moving itself and makes the correct choices to run particular programs, you can bet your last dollar that you've been hacked and that your mouse is being controlled by humans.

The hackers who can take control of your computer in this way can start working in your system at any time. However they will usually wait until it has been idle for a long time (eg, during the early hours of the morning) before they start using it, which is why it is important that you turn off your computer at night and disconnect it physically from the internet.

Hackers will use their ability to open and close programs remotely to break into your bank accounts and transfer money, buy and sell your stocks and shares, and do all sorts of other nefarious deeds in order to deprive you of your treasure.

What to do: If your computer suddenly swings into action some night, you should turn it off as soon as possible. However, before you do so, try to find out what the hacker is interested in and what they are trying to do. If you have a digital camera handy or a smartphone, take a few pictures of the screen to document what the hacker is doing.

After you have closed it down, disconnect your computer from the internet and call for professional help. To solve this problem you will need expert help from an online computer maintenance firm.

But before you call for help, use another computer that is known to be good, to change all your log-in details for your online accounts. Check your bank accounts, stockbroker accounts and so on. If you discover that you have lost money or other valuables, call the police and make a complaint.

You have to take this kind of attack seriously and the only option you should choose for recovery if a complete clean-out and re-installation of your operating system and applications.

But before you do so, if you have suffered financial losses, give a forensic team access to your computer so they can check exactly what took place. You may need a report from them to recover your monetary losses from your insurer, banker, broker or online merchant.

[6] Anti-virus program, Task Manager or Registry Editor disabled and won't restart

Stuff can happen, so one of these three applications could go wrong on its own. Two of them might go wrong at the same time in a million-to-one coincidence. But when all three go wrong together...

In fact, a lot of malware does try to protect itself by degrading these three applications so either they won't start or they start in a reduced state.

What to do: you cannot know what really happened, so you should perform a complete restoration of your computer system.

The above are just six fairly common signs that you have been hacked. There are plenty more.

These include: money missing from your bank account; your internet searches being redirected to places to which you do not want to go; being plagued by pop-up ads when you visit websites that normally don't generate them; and so on.

Once you've been hacked you can never really know for sure what's going on inside your system. A compromised system can never be fully trusted.

WHAT TO DO IF YOUR COMPUTER IS HACKED

Hacking has been one of the serious dangers posed by the technological developments in the communication industry. The truth is that hacking has been threatening humans from a long time now but due to developments in communications and the dawn of internet, hacking has gain a new life in the form of internet hacking. Internet makes it possible for hacking to reach new heights. Here's a definition of hacking:

What is Hacking?

Hacking is the process of making changes to a program in order to achieve your goal aloof from the original creator's objective. A hacker is someone who engages in these activities. Hacker's are usually expert programmers. In simple words, it is the process of making use of other's resources for your own purpose without their approval. It's no different than stealing.

Computer Hacked: What to do

Is your computer hacked? What to do now? The truth is that computer hacking is so dreaded that it can make anybody nervous. The dangers of hacking make it so frightening that it is a nightmare for any computer user. The dangers range from the theft of personal information to the misuse of resources. Imagine an intruder accessing your personal information and using it for his own false objectives. The picture is not so beautiful. Not only individual computer users but even giants are not safe. So what should you do if you're actually made a victim by hackers. Here's a little checklist:

The first thing you should do is to turn off your computer system. This will give you time to think and get your nerves. This will also save your computer from further damage.

Backup your important files on an external hard drive to ensure that you do not lose any precious data in case your computer dies.

The second step is one of the most important of the process. The second step involves the shutting off of all of all your internet connection. This step will cut you off from the hackers reach and protect you from further penetration of the hacker. However, do not think of it as the permanent solution your problem as this will only protect you from hacker's further intrusion but the running processes will continue.

If your computer is hacked, then now you need to scan your computer with an antivirus software to scan your entire memory and detect infected files. Repair them with your antivirus software or just delete them.

Some hackers even delete or disable your security programs. If that's the case with you than go for wiping your whole memory. Format your hard drive and reinstall your operating system. This is a painful step but the most effective one. I recommend consulting a professional first.

If your computer is hacked, its important to hold your nerves in order to choose the best possible solution for your problem. Hacking is a nuisance. With these simple basic steps, I hope you'll be able to recover from any danger the intruder has posed.

ETHICAL HACKING SALARY

Those who run an online business, or work with computers in some other capacity, are at risk from unscrupulous hackers. But what if you were able to step in and stop them? An ethical hacking salary should certainly be rewarding enough, and demand has never been higher. The fact is, there are a significant number of people who make it their hobby or business to break in to online accounts, or websites, and to alter, steal or remove data.

This practice is known as hacking. Naturally, hacking will be viewed by most as a complete violation of privacy, and not to be accepted in any way, shape or form. However, a good number of people fail to see that there can be good derived out of learning how to hack. Know your enemy springs to mind!

There are many large and small companies looking to hire hackers. After all, who knows better about IT security and vulnerabilities than a seasoned hacker? When hired, their task is to make sure that all of their employers programs and websites remain secure from hacking attempts. They can test the security (by attempting to hack as a would-be attacker,) looking for anything exploitable. If found, they are to report their findings to the appropriate programmer so the issue can be fixed.

There are actually several job openings for hackers in many companies. And with the ethical hacking salary being quite high, it can be very appealing indeed. These people are normally experts in the field of computer security and are well trained to hack into all manner of systems. People with such expertise are very helpful to companies and can potentially save them millions of dollars, much embarrassment and potential lost of reputation.

The ethical hacking salary within most companies is comfortably high (relatively speaking) and rightfully so because as aforementioned, they are saving the company a lot of money, and require specialist skills. There are even training courses available for people who want to be a hacker. Choosing to specialize in this field is quite profitable and can lead to a comfortable lifestyle and stable employment.

People live in a time where we all are becoming more and more dependent on computers. More companies are starting to depend heavily on their computers and any hacking done can cause serious damage. In the near future, ethical hacking jobs will become more common and the ethical hacking salary will be even higher.

Being paid to hack is quite enticing to many for several reasons. It is not just the desirable ethical hacking salary, it is also the challenge the role represents. Further, when you add in the fun factor which hacking clearly has to many, it is not at all hard to imagine why those with the knowledge would go for such a career.

In short, hacking is often seen as a sport by many, and can be outright fun! So why not get paid to do it?

WIRELESS HACKS

Just in case you are running out of things to worry about and would appreciate a fresh supply, you may want to consider the likelihood of a hacker hacking into your wireless devices and meddling with the controls of your vehicle, your pacemaker or even your blender.

Yep, it is all possible - that and more, according to techno-goddess and talk show host, Kim Komando. The "wireless advantage' is proving advantageous to more than just the consumer - and with some of these devices, the stakes are higher than they would be if a hacker gained access to your PC. Think "life threatening" in some cases.

Pacemakers

Pacemakers are life saving devices in that they intervene should the heart beat drop to a certain low level. In the past, surgery was needed when a pacemaker required reprogramming. However, many of today's pacemakers contain a wireless feature that allows the cardiology team to reprogram the device via radio waves. In 2008, US researchers at Medical Device Security Center determined that "black hats" could hack these unencrypted radio waves and take control of the pacemaker. Once in control, the hackers could turn off the pacemaker completely or deliver an electrical shock strong enough to lead to cardiac arrest.

To date, I am not aware that this type of hack has ever occurred outside the research lab. The medical researchers said that the "hacking kit" would cost about $30,000, would require skill and expertise to operate and would only work if the hacker and the hackee were physically close to one another.

Given the above limitations, this doesn't sound like a big threat to most pacemaker users. However, Wired.com postulated that hacks of this kind could pose a threat to prominent individuals such as government officials and politicians.

In November of 2009, Swiss researchers announced plans to investigate ultrasound waves as a means of preventing pacemaker hacks.

Vehicles

Contemporary vehicles such as the Dodge Grand Caravan and others come with built-in Wi-Fi. Should the Wi-Fi be hacked, the invaders would have the ability to interfere with the control of your vehicle - including disabling the breaks or stopping your automobile while it is in motion. Picture this happening during fast traffic conditions or during rush hour and you get a sense of the danger. Komando recommends turning off the Wi-Fi while it is not in use.

Not only that, researchers at the University of Washington and the University of California San Diego used a laptop computer and specially written software to hack into the controls of two makes of 2009 sedans. The laptop was connected to the on-board diagnostics port, a feature that is mandated by law in the USA. New Scientist magazine reported that the researchers turned off the engine and disabled the brakes while the car traveled at 65 kilometers per hour. The scientists declined to name the makes and models of the vehicles tested.

Although these researchers used a connected laptop in the experiment, it would be possible, they say, to use hardware that would allow remote control. They also reported taking control of a car using wireless signals and operating it over the Internet.

As with the pacemakers, no known vehicle hacks have occurred outside of research conditions, and to do would require considerable skill. Nevertheless, the automotive industry would be wise to develop security patches before hacks occur.

Home Appliances

Home appliances - such as your blender - can be hacked if they are connected to an automated home system. Komando points out that most appliances have security features that can be turned on or off - but comments that the consumer rarely bothers to activate the security. Her recommendation is to ensure that the all security features are put into operation.

As for the likelihood of hacking into a home network, a quick Google search revealed multiple web sites providing hacking information, tips and hacking kits. One even provides a video demonstration entitled "How to Hack into WEP Encrypted Wireless Networks."

Hacking a wireless network is hardly new. In 2004, a man in Michigan pleaded guilty to various counts of fraud after he hacked a wireless network at a Lowe's store with the plan of stealing credit card numbers recorded in the main computer systems. The hacker discovered a poorly protected LAN while performing random scanning for open connections, an activity known as war driving.

Other Wireless Gadgets

Other wireless gadgets, including Smart Phones (DROIDS) and wireless printers are vulnerable to hacking.

Once in your Smart Phone, the hacker has full access and control to anything in your telephone. Komando claims that hackers typically gain access in much the same way they do with your PC. It's likely to be through a text message or email offering you a special service or APP. Use the same cautions you use on your desktop computer.

As for the wireless functionality of your printer, despite manufacturer stipulations to the contrary, these devices have less security than your PC. Komando recommends using a regular printer cable hookup at home, especially if you live in an apartment or a condominium.

Why?

So why would anyone want to hack into your wireless devices? I do not profess to understand the criminal mind, but I would guess the motivations are the same as they are for any other crime: profit, fun or spite.

THE FEAR OF BEING HACKED AND ATTACKED ON FACEBOOK

In this chapter, I will be taking the time to talk to you about Facebook hacks and viruses, the reasons these are not just annoying but very dangerous, and how to personally stay diligent to avoid them. This , I hope will be most helpful and provide you valuable insight on keeping your personal information and friends safe! Spread the word!

First off, hacks and viruses have become so common in the internet world that they are no longer looked at as "threats" by the general public and are seen as mere annoyances. This is a false thought; hacks and viruses are created for the sole purpose of getting yours, your friends, and your family's personal information. Have you ever been the victim of a hack or virus?

How long did it take for you to take that computer to a specialist? Before you took it to a specialist how many times did you check your email, Facebook, or bank account? Although not all hacks and viruses can see the info you use directly, how do you know which ones can? So why would you take the risk?

Why do they want my personal information? In the real world, people use scams for the sole purpose of getting money. This is the same concept in the world of internet. The difference is that the internet provides a lot more tactics to get that information as well as a lot more ways to use it. With the dawn of the internet came a whole new world that was exciting to everyone, when in reality it can be the single most frightening part of our everyday lives! Why? To take it back to a Facebook level, if I randomly add you as a friend and you have no idea who I am, you still accept me as a friend because everyone's friendly in social networking. At this point all I have to do is take your name and your birthday should you have it on your Facebook account, or even more helpful, your list of relatives. I can find all of your addresses you have ever had, and from here I can take all this information and use it to get your background report and social security number. Now that I have this info, my possibilities are endless. I can now pretend to be you and start working on getting credit cards and what not in your name. To make matters worse, most people use the same email and password for everything they do, and if you show me this personal email on your Facebook profile I am then one quick program away from accessing everything you everything you have like credit cards and bank accounts. Oh, and I can do all this in less than an hour's time!If this is what the average Joe can do then imagine what the experts are capable of!

Although Facebook is a big, notable company it is still a young pup in the internet world. It has only been with use since 2004. This makes Facebook a huge target for online hacking and viruses. Don't miss understand me, Facebook itself is very secure and a force to be reckoned with. The action happens on a personal profile level on a day to day basis from friends to friends, and a lot of time happens without you ever realizing it happened. Social networking sites such as Facebook are big targets due to the amount of information within profiles and the simple fact that it is supposed to be a trusted network of friends. We mindlessly click on anything given to us by a trusted friend or relative, so if they can take that account it can spider web into a gold mine.

What can I do to protect myself?

Just as the darker side of the internet has options, so do we! There are many ways to help avoid these hacks and viruses. First off, when it comes to Facebook or any social networks, keep in mind your antivirus has no way of protecting your account, it can only protect your computer and is never 100% effective! Protecting yourself on the internet is just that: "protecting yourself".

Take caution when adding new friends, take pride enough in your personal information not to put it all out there, and only put what you feel is necessary or important.

Emails and passwords are another huge way to protect you. The key here is to use as many difference passwords as possible and try not to use the same one twice. This can limit the hack or virus' access to just that one item instead of a mess your personal accounts. It is also a very good idea to keep sites that have very sensitive information such as bank accounts and credit card sites under a separate email only used for those items, but remember to keep the passwords different. The reason behind having multiple email accounts is based on the fact that if your single email account is taken then the individual who has that account can have all your passwords send to that account for reset. For security reasons, in today's world you can never have enough email accounts. This method is very helpful, but it cannot stop the problem on its own. In order to help yourself prevent hacks and viruses, you must be very cautious about what you click on or look at on your Facebook account and on the internet in general.

What do I look for and how do I know not to click on it?

When these hack or virus attacks happen on Facebook, they usually affect a lot of people and travel from friend to friend by users clicking links. One of the big tell-tale signs of Facebook messages, wall links, or news links that may contain a hack or virus is that although there are many different versions and always new ones, each one will use the same message or post to attract you. This means that if you see a bunch of your friends post or email the same exact message that this is more than likely a hack or virus, and you will contract it should you click the link. The creator of the hack or virus wants you to see these as a popular chain letter, video, or link. Your options with these situations are to: 1. Not click on the link 2. Report the link 3. Message your friend or relative back and ask if they intended to send this message. In most cases accounts that get hacked or viruses still leave the original user control over the account and they go on using Facebook as if nothing happened, so it is fairly safe to ask before you click.

What if I have been hacked or have a Facebook virus and how do I know?

First off, if you know your account was compromised, quickly change your password to your email address followed by changing the password to your Facebook account. It is best done in this order to prevent immediate reccurrences. The best way to tell if this has happened to you is to regularly check your Facebook email and profile for any emails or posts that you did not make yourself. If you see any of these then please change your email password immediately followed by your Facebook password.

There is no sure-fire way to stop these attacks; there are only ways to be diligent in protecting yourself. Remember to use caution with your personal information, be careful of who you add as a friend, and watch out for suspicious behavior. Keep in mind that if you have any doubt you should ask the sender to make sure it really is the person you trust and that they intended to send it.

To provide a little motivation into why you should be diligent on this topic, as I said earlier the goal is to get your information or pretend to be you to make money. It is the way they do it that requires you to be cautious not only for yourself but for others. Some of these hacks or viruses will try to get you to download something that can either take your information or pester you until you buy an item, which then gives them control of your money. Others will recommend that you or your friends buy a product that then steals the card numbers used to "purchase" the item. The scariest of all ways though is hidden in the personal bonds we have with our families and friends. Some of these hacks and viruses will contact your friends and family telling them you are in trouble and need them to send x amount of money to get to safety or some other similar scenario. Unsafe practices can cause your profile to be the doorway to conning your friends and family out of their money. So please, if not for yourself, be careful for the sake of others you trust and care about!

POINTS TO CONSIDER IN SECURING WEBSITES AND CREATING VIRTUAL KEYWORDS AGAINST HACKING PASSWORDS

As technology advances overtime, it has been positively used to help promote businesses, products or services as well as enhancing websites. But at some point, it has been negatively also used by culprits to "crash" websites and businesses even hacking passwords to the software. As the increasing number of cases of hackers used to hack websites or malware attack reported in news, bad impact brought about by technology is also constantly rise. System hacking is one of the most common issues nowadays. That is why to settle this problem, security concerns and issues have been tackled because Internet is now widely use by people from all walks of life. Whether a business is large or small, proper attention should be given like protecting and safeguarding all their network software against corrupt hackers. That is why it is vitally important that every system operators or administrators must use a distinctive password that can't be hacked either by an ordinary destroyer or professional hackers. As early as possible, one should be vigilant from unexpected hackers.

Basically, a person who does hacking commonly destroys software and other computer networks in order to gain more money or only encourage doing the challenge. To avoid unnecessary accidents like hacking passwords, you should take some precautionary measures not only for your systems protection but also for your own safety as well. That is why the need of powerful password is a must for privacy and security of your website. It ensures you the confidentiality and safety of your save data. It is a great responsibility of the user to make a password as unique as possible in a way that complicated to guess or to be discovered by anyone.

To avoid hacking on your password, the following are the points to consider when creating a virtual keyword.

1. When creating a password, you should enter mix information like in your credit card, bank account or any assume a name that is extraordinary.

2. A second good advice is to use alphanumeric, a combination of numbers and letters even mix with symbols. For a higher security, at least two letters that you enter should be in uppercase.

3. Creating a password should be hard or rare to be guess wherein other programs and even other people can't quickly discover.

4. A word should not an existing name regardless of any language used.

5. Don't use your initial names, date of your birth and other common words because it can be easily guessed.

6. Don't use other older accounts.

7. The password to enter should be 5-digit or more for additional security.

8. Do not try to use usual passwords.

9. Having two or more accounts for your email, you must use another password. Be sure that you will memorize your entire password to avoid failures.

10. The last but not the least tip is that try to have a list base on your common used programs like notes, excel or word to all your websites, mail boxes or either through your subscriptions and mail back to its right place or location. Your password and username use should be neat and properly organize so that you can immediately use it.

After making a virtual password into your account, should also take consider on how to secure your valuable website against from accidental attacks and cruel hackers. The following are the pointers to consider:

1. Install a virus protection on your software to have a complete safeguarding on your website.

2. Modify and transform your password always by selecting alphanumeric words. To avoid committing of failures, be sure that

you have a list for every password and username that you made.

3. Keep updating on your use safety measure patches to avid harmful viruses that might enter in your systems like Trojans.

4. Connect to Google webmaster wherein it will help or assist you to learn on different hacking endeavors.

5. Lastly, you should always have back-ups to restore the date you save.

IPHONE HACKS & SOFTWARE

With the iPhone news of the Apple launch, the number of iPhone hacks has increased exponentially and a great deal of energy has been put into working through the iPhone software to find where the passwords and the "glue" is for a number of apps. The "Holy Grail" at the moment is iPhone unlocking.

iPhone unlocking is in fact most requested hack, and unlocking means that the iPhone can be used on any network and not just AT&T's. There have been a couple of claims to have managed this iPhone hack ultimate but so far it's all just rumors though it seems that a couple are indeed getting close and have managed to gain ownership of the file system. Sieving through the iPhone software and especially the gif images that are embedded seems to be the number preoccupation of any self respecting iPhone hack merchant around the globe.

One writer at GigaOM claims that they have gotten all the iPhone functions working except the telephone, voicemail and text features. To be honest I don't see the point in all of this, getting an iPhone hack to unlock the beast is not going to be of much use unless you use the iPhone overseas and on top of that you'll have no 3G support.

Where I do see a value in getting the iPhone software opened up, is that once we have the iPhone unlocked then being able to use the device as an ultimately portable minicomputer working over a wifi network then we have something that's going to be useful.

On the iPhone news grapevine, it's not just iPhone hacks that are streaming in thick and fast, there are also a series of full-blown web apps which I have to say is pretty impressive - well done guys! Probably the best one at the moment is the iPhone hack "iChat for iPhone" which provides you with IM capability on AIM. More than that, the iPhone software source is available for this hack and you can host it on your own machine. If you are really serious about keeping up-to-date with the latest in iPhone unlocking and iPhone hacks then check out the iPhone Dev Wiki that seems to me to be the closest to getting an iPhone unlocking hack.

iPhone software that you can download onto your new iPhone can be found at iPhone Applications on the web. Here you'll find all iPhone software and applications such as iWeather and more games than you can shake a stick at. Unfortunately, until we get iPhone hack that will open up the iPhone to third party applications we are going to have to make do with Apple iPhone software that we're allowed to play with at the moment.

SECURING YOUR COMPUTER AND PERSONAL ACCOUNTS FROM HACKING ATTEMPTS

High-profile celebrities, multinational corporations, and military institutions all share one thing in common: They were all compromised before or have their accounts and networks infiltrated by computer hackers. However, never assume that hackers only aim at prominent and valuable targets. Hacking of computers and Internet accounts for personal and financial information is becoming more prevalent and more and more computer users and Web surfers are at risk of falling victim to them. News media has recently reported of increasing attempts by hackers to take control of e-mail accounts and social network webpages such as Twitter and Facebook. More and more computer users have enlisted the help of purchased or free antivirus solutions and professional advice to help them deal with hacking intrusions.

Before we continue on with this article, we will need to define clearly what "hacking" really means and what actions do it constitutes or covers. Hacking is the general term that is used to identify attempts by persons or users to make off with your e-mail records, computer system, network connections, and Internet security settings. Simply put, it is any effort by hackers and other shady individuals to use the Web or local network to intrude in your PC or laptop and steal your important information.

To the accomplished hacker or to any computer expert in general, hacking can be a relatively basic action that can be accomplished with minimum effort. With the right skill set and attitude, basically anyone can get into computer and Internet accounts illegally and pilfer away critical personal information. A computer user can be called a hacker if he or she somehow gets the e-mail account password or Facebook account name of other individuals and uses them to steal personal information. They often take advantage of the fact that many passwords can easily be guessed; many computer and Internet users sadly only use "1234" or the term "password" as their password for important personal computer and online accounts. E-mail accounts and addresses are often targeted by hackers because they are often used as access points to your confidential Internet data. Hackers can also use other more complicated means and tools to gain control of computer files and make off with critical personal data such as Trojan horses, spam, spyware, and phishing; oftentimes, they can bypass the protective screen that is provided by most paid or free antivirus applications.

There are some hacking techniques that are so complicated and difficult to understand that only professional computer users and experts are able to follow them. They are used by skilled hackers to infiltrate and compromise the computerized networks of private corporations and government institutions, despite the high level of security that are provided for them.

So you come to realize the importance of protecting your computer and accounts from hacking attempts; you now ask yourself, "How can I better secure my computer?" You can easily realize this by strengthening your Internet security against hacking attempts and malware intrusions. To do this, you should first devise solid passwords for each of your e-mail and social media accounts. Secure passwords are those that contain lengthy and apparently haphazard sets of numbers, letters and special symbols and characters such as "&" and "@."

REALITY HACKING

Supernatural and Occult has always captured the imagination of the human mind. There are numerous cases where specific beliefs have been exploited by people for wrong purposes. It is important to understand where to draw a line. While It is easy to slip into debates related to religion and global issues, we will focus on an example of reality hacking and see how one can be exploited using a belief. The subject itself is controversial in nature, so it's best we kept aside the moral values and ethics for a later discussion.

Before we start, lets understand what hacking is and what a system is. Most people say, hacking is about stealing passwords and getting the root or something similar. And a system is any computer or network which we want to hack. But in true sense, hacking is not just about passwords. It's about improvising a process or taking advantage of a system as a whole. A system consists of people, process and technology.

So, even the entire company is a system. The way nature operates is a form of system. Even the way you do your daily routine and spend time with your family is a system. And hacking can be applied just anywhere, by studying it carefully. This view is generally known as reality hacking, and is similar to the final climax of Matrix, where Neo finally believes in himself and sees everything, including himself as a part of Matrix.

Occult science in everyday life.

How many times have you read or seen people reading the daily astrology column in newspapers? or, how many times have you shown your hand to a common friend or a hand-reading expert to know the future? How much of it do you believe really?

Some examples:

In India, almost every marriage is done only if the stars match. You would face considerable resistance from old grannies and mothers in getting married to the girl you like, if the kundalis1 do not match. Imagine, a small astrological chart can actually determine if your family approves your relationship or not!

The home interiors, design and furniture is largely determined by Vaastu Shastra2 in many Indian homes. Even today, new apartments or flats are rejected if they do not satisfy the aspects of Vaastu! So if you are a builder, you have a slightly better chance of selling your newly constructed buildings / homes if you promote them as designed as per Vaastu Shastra in certain parts of India!

Huge donations are given in name of Poojaa3 or Homam4 which are held almost every month some place or other to ward of evil spirits, seek blessings of god and bring peace and harmony. The revenue generated by these donations qualify the religious bodies to be listed in Stock markets! For example, the annual turnover of Tirumala

Tirupati Devasthanam (One of the largest religious bodies in India) is over 135,093,956.32 USD! Not to mention reserves.

Again, some of the largest riots and acts of violence are due to differences between religious communities. We have witnessed thousands of people being killed on the name of religion and justice. As they say, even today most people are judged by the color of their skin.

People and Belief

As we saw from the above examples, it does not matter if you believe in any forms of occult or religion. What matters is many people do. And this belief is the single largest factor to utilize it for your advantage. Over many years i have noticed that gaining trust is easiest when you share your victim's belief or add weight to it by your experiences or stories.

It is not hard to find out if your victim can be exploited or not. One can start with a simple sociological game like 'nowadays' or 'Ain't it awful' and quickly move towards stating a personal problem that got resolved due to a certain practice5. For instance, one can say "You know, I was thinking of purchasing this plot, but luckily I had been to this astrologer and you won't believe it, he said I should not make the purchase as it was not a good period. Just yesterday I came to know that the plot was actually having a lot of legal issues and that it had being seized." Depending on the person or place, stories like this might actually work. If you sound convincing enough, then your victim asks for the address and decides to test the astrologer out.

If you can recollect your days at college, there would be at least one guy who would have claimed to read hands, and all girls would flock around him to ask the same stupid questions, "When will i get married?"

"Will I go abroad?" "Will my husband be good looking?" "Will i get first class in my exams?" or more family oriented ones like "Will I always take care of my mother and father?"; "What about my mothers health?" or "Will i get a job soon?" and things like that.

To tell you how serious this can be, once out of frustration I replied to a girl that she will have two marriages and that she would get a divorce from her first husband within six months. Before I could realize, she fainted out of shock and fell down the staircase. It was very difficult for me to later tell her that it was just a joke and that she would actually be happy in a single long lasting marriage. This is not an isolated case.

People believe "predictions" when given in a right environment and though most of them can act as "self-fulfilling prophecies", it is natural to be concerned when you are warned of danger.

Now how can ones belief help you in hacking? In any business, if crucial sales professionals or account managers leave a company or are not available for active follow up, they will lose a great amount of business to competitors. Is there any way we can "hack" into a TAM or pre-sales professionals mind and make them not report to office for a few days for a possible business advantage?

A Real Corporate Sabotage example using Occult

In Mumbai, at Andheri, there are over 3000 companies with corporate offices. On any given working day, there are over 120 odd IT security Pre-sales guys trying to sell their services in various sectors. In such a cut throat competition, it is vital that presentations or proposals are given on time. It is also obvious that not all can qualify for certain jobs and that only few competitors remain in the end.

Company X wanted the deal at all costs. What can it do to prevent company Y from winning this order? It was then that they tried out a simple plan. Krishna (let's say) was a pre-sales guy working with company Y. He used to commute daily from Dombivili to Andheri by local train via Dadar. Company X studied the daily activity of Krishna for a few days and strategically sent a Sadhu early morning at his area.

Sadhu6

When Krishna came out as usual for going to office, the Sadhu came forward and asked for a rupee but instead stopped haphazardly and gave him a cold spooky stare before saying "Your death is near! you are going die in a train accident in less than a week" (In reality, it was very dramatic). Saying this he gave a "you-are-doomed" laugh and quickly walked away.

Now what do you think would be the effect? Surprised, Krishna paused for a few seconds and regained his composure before moving to his work place as usual. After two days, company X sent another Sadhu who "accidentally" crossed Krishna's path and suddenly froze before giving him the look.

This time the Sadhu said "Son, your life is in danger. Stay at home and recite the hanuman chalisaa7 everyday if you want the danger to pass away". Blessing him, the Sadhu started moved away chanting mantras. But this time Krishna quickly called him and asked what the danger was. The Sadhu replied that the period was extremely bad for him for he has not fulfilled a promise made to god. And the only way out was to stay indoors for a week or so chanting "hanuman chalisaa" 108 times a day. During this time he should not travel anywhere as it would surely put him in danger of losing his life.

Even now, the company X did not know how Krishna would react to all this. Krishna thanked the Sadhu, gave him a 50 Rupee note and moved towards office. But soon the two separate incidents of being warned of death put Krishna in the desired state of mind. By the time he reached Dadar, he changed his mind and went back home instead of office. In the next few hours Krishna called in "sick".

With an able pre-sales guy not attending office due to "sudden illness" had its toll on the overall aggressiveness of the business of company Y. Even though company Y sent out another sales guy to handle the job, he did not share the same rapport and comfort as Krishna did with his customers. In less than a week, company X was able to close a crucial deal from an energy based company that was worth over INR .85,00,000/- because of less competition.

SECURE WORDPRESS SITES

Often times you leave our WordPress sites completely unsecured and hope for the best. You don't bother to configure security measures on your site and go through the extra work. You think - "No hacker is going to notice my site among the millions of WordPress sites on the web!". This hope can be your downfall.

Hackers these days uses "hack bots", to put it simply these are automated hacking machines searching the web (e.g. through Google) and collecting millions of sites for hacking target. Once collected these bots attempt hacking on this list of sites and if your site is on the list and is not secured, you are likely to get hacked automatically. So, as you can see hackers don't have to target you specifically for you to get hacked.

Once you are hacked, you panic, you feel the pain & fear of possibly losing all you hard work and even often times a source of income, but it's too late. Your site is already messed up, your data is compromised and you don't know if you can restore it.

In many cases hacked sites are restorable by removing the hacker's malicious code restored to original state, but in many cases site is damaged to such extent you just have to start all over again or just abandon the site altogether.

Why go through this when you can prevent this from happening in the first place? Secure your WordPress site right from the beginning. I understand security is a complex task to handle, in which case you should hire a WordPress security expert to handle the task. There are lot reliable security professionals out there who you help you with this.

Where do you find them? Browse or search through freelancing sites site Freelance, Fiverr, Odesk and where you can post your own project for free. On the other hand, on sites like Fiverr you can just search for security related gigs and hire your preferred expert to work on your site.

How do you know who is reliable? Usually on these sites you will be able to view the user's ratings and feedbacks left by other people who hired them Read the reviews learn about their previous work.

On Fiverr you can also talk to the user before you hire them and this will help you get an idea about the attitude and level of professionalism of the user.

Either you do it yourself or use an expert, you must secure WordPress sites. There is no point in saving a few bucks and losing hundreds when your site gets hacked. So, if you haven't secured your WordPress sites yet, go ahead and secure it now and you will be a lot safer out in the web. It will bring you peace of mind as well.

BASICS OF ETHICAL HACKING AND PENETRATION TESTING

Do you want your business to have a secure system? Protect it from dubious characters who want to steal sensitive documents by hiring a reputable information security specialist. They can provide ethical hacking, penetration testing, and Payment Card Industry (PCI) training and consulting. Here is more information about what this is and what it can do for your company.

What is an information security specialist?

Another term for an information security specialist is a computer security specialist. This expert is responsible for protecting the computer system from threats. These threats can be internal or external in nature. Other than, private businesses, the specialist provides services for government agencies and educational institutions.

The need for these skilled professionals continues to grow. This is because threats to computer systems and networks develop rapidly along with technological developments. Due to this, the specialist must continue to upgrade his or her level of knowledge. He or she must also increase arsenal of useful tools, applications, and systems.

A basic security measure involves the control of passwords. A computer security specialist may require the members of the company to change their password frequently. This reduces the chances of unauthorized access to confidential programs, networks, or databases.

Who would I protect my business from?

Usually, the most dangerous risk to any computer network comes from outside sources. The specialist puts up firewalls for hackers. He or she regularly installs programs that have automatic alerts when there is any attempt to infiltrate the system. You can even find high-tech programs that can point out where the hacker is by identifying the internet protocol address of the intruder.

Two popular services offered by computer specialists are ethical hacking and penetration testing.

Ethical hacking and Penetration testing 101

Skilled computer experts usually perform ethical hacking. They use their programming skills to know the weaknesses in computer systems. While you can find non-ethical hackers abusing the vulnerabilities for personal gain, the ethical hacker evaluates and points them out, then suggests changes to strengthen the system. Computer experts keep systems and information safe with their ethical hacking services.

Most IT specialists consider ethical hacking as plain hacking because it still makes use of knowledge of computer systems in an attempt to crash or penetrate them. Most business owners consider it ethical because of its purpose, which is to increase the security in systems.

Penetration testing, on the other hand, is a kind of security evaluation done on a computer system. This involves a person trying to hack into the system. The goal of this service is to find out if someone with malicious intent can enter the system. Penetration testing can reveal what programs or applications hackers can access once they penetrate the system. There are many firms and online businesses offering penetration testing. This is highly-recommended, as damage to a computer system caused by a hostile attack can be costly to repair.

Most companies are required to have penetration testing. Compliance with the standard can seem difficult at first, but you can find many companies that have enough experience to help businesses meet the requirements at all levels.

HOW TO PREVENT SOMEONE FROM HACKING INTO YOUR EMAIL ACCOUNT

Email hacking is a very common practice. I was amazed at the number of sites that offer to teach you how to hack someone's email. This is a terrible practice and not only is it an invasion of privacy but it can be used for a variety of illegal practices.

In the news today: "Attorney Appeals Decision in Palin Email Hacking" as reported on NewsChannel5.com, a young man has been found guilty of hacking into Sarah Palin's email account during the presidential campaign. His sentence can be 21 months in jail! This is certainly no laughing matter. For those folks who have had their email hacked... there is nothing funny about it. What can you do to prevent your email from being hacked?

1. Never give personal or account information in an email.

Most email accounts are hacked by 'phishing'. Phishing is when you receive an email from what appears to be a legitimate site and it asks you to click on links or enter personal/private information. NEVER do this, because if you do, you have just given the hacker the personal info they need to access' your accounts, like banking or credit card details.

These hackers can be very clever and they work hard to make the 'phishing site' appear like the legitimate website. If you receive an email from your bank and it asks you to click on a link within the email...don't do it. If it asks for account info...don't do it. If you know the website address of your bank, type it in your browser. Then login and you will see if there are any messages for you. Any legitimate bank will never ask you for personal account details in an email. Alternately, you can call your bank, using the phone number on your bank statements or in the phone book. Never use the one on the email.

2. Use an Internet browser that has 'phishing filters'. A phishing filter is a software program that works to identify fraudulent websites which attempt to represent the legitimate sites. Firefox and Windows 7 are just two of the browsers that incorporate phishing filters.

3. Check for filters in your email account. If for example you use Gmail, you can login and go to your settings and then check your filters. See if you recognize them as ones you set up. If not, get rid of it.

4. Never click on links within an email unless you know the page it is taking you to. I have found a very useful tool called 'Cooliris' and it is a plugin which allows you to preview a page without clicking on the link. Not only does it keep you from clicking on a link you don't want to go to, it also saves time by not having to open another webpage or tab to view the destination page of the link.

YOUR EMPLOYEES MUST BE AS KNOWLEDGEABLE IN HACKING MATTERS

Hacking is one of those terms dropped in conversations to prove management is on top of the issues related to computer security. Computer security breaches are reported everyday and occur in even the most tightly controlled environments simply because people are not thoroughly trained in how to identify them or mission critical systems have points where security is missing. Operations where you would think all precautions have been taken find themselves embarrassed when someone steals important information for the purpose of committing a crime.

As recently as November 2008, it was reported a prison inmate gained access to employee online files containing personal information using a computer that was not intended to have access to the internet. The programmers thought access to the internet had been prevented. But "not intended to" doesn't mean much when using integrated computer systems, because hackers can find ways to get around portals that are guarded. It's like securing the front and back doors of a building while leaving the side windows unlocked.

Understanding the Problem

In the case of the prison inmate, he accessed employee files using a thin client on the prison server. Though the server was not programmed to allow internet access, the inmate cleverly entered the internet using stolen username and password information from employee files and uncovering a portal in the software used by inmates for legal research.

If an inmate can hack into a prison system with sophisticated security systems meant to guard the public, it is clear there must be multi-levels of security which notify those monitoring the system that an attempt to break-in is happening. The goal is to catch and stop the breach before any information is accessed. In other words, a well designed security system will have two features:

* Security systems preventing penetration

* Trained employees with the knowledge to recognize the signs of a hacking attempt and possible entry points for hacking

You can hire an internet security service to assess your security and design a penetration preventing application, but the employees using the system day-in and day-out need to be knowledgeable in the ways system attackers operate and how they locate and abuse vulnerable systems.

It Takes One to Know One

Basically, you teach your employees how to be hackers so they can prevent hacking. Courses which are intended to teach employees about internet security systems focus on how hackers exploit systems and how to recognise attempts. They also learn how countermeasures work and return to the workplace ready to implement organisational-specific measures to protect computer systems.

If the prison had established security levels which provided notification someone was trying to access employee files through a software program and then prevented that access, there would have been no breach. It is important to make sure your employees are knowledgeable so they can identify possible vulnerability, recognise hacking attempts, know how to use exploit tools, and can develop countermeasures.

Many times hackers make it all the way to sensitive information because employees don't recognise hacking activity. There is an old expression that says, "It takes one to know one." In the world of hacking, it takes an employee highly trained in hacking to know a hacker. But the payoff for this kind of training is immeasurable as company assets are protected.

RUNESCAPE HACKS

If you are reading this chapter you are most likely looking for Runescape hacks and tips. You want to get as many Runescape Items and make as much free Runescape gold as possible with the least effort. I am sorry to say to you then that the only Runescape hacks that work are those that get you hacked.

All over the internet, most Runescape forums, message boards and even in the game itself you will find Runescape scammers. These are people who will tell you that they will be able to make you wealthy and give you loads of items. The only thing they want from you is your username and password. Whatever you do, do not give this to them. They are users who will login on your account go the Runescape bank, take out all your items and gold and deposit it on their own account. At this point they both change your password and leave you without a Runescape account or if they are somewhat "kind" they will return the account to you.

What about Runescape hacks I can download for free? Again, don't! Often these Runescape autominers, auto fighters or item duplicators are trojans and key loggers. This means they take control over your computer and find out what your Runescape password is and then hack it.

How can I protect myself?

Make your Runescape password long, and use numbers, characters and capital letters.

Only use this password for Runescape.com (the game), nowhere else. It has happened that Runescape users have signed up for Runescape forums with the same username and password and then got hacked.

Do not download any Runescape Hacks. They are all scams. Why? If you had a program that would make you millions in Runescape would you give it out for free? You wouldn't!

Do never give out your password or any details that can lead to someone knowing it.

Be careful in Runescape, there are a lot of scammers trying to get your Runescape gold and items.

BUY A HACK ATTACK PITCHING MACHINE

If you want your team to really take it's hitting to the next level, it's time to consider incorporating a Hack Attack pitching machine into your practice routine. Used from high school and college teams to the professional big league players, this machine is a sturdy, well-built powerhouse of a pitcher that will rival even the best human efforts.

What Is a Hack Attack Pitching Machine?

It's an exceptional baseball pitching machine with a unique three-wheel design that, allows the hitter to see the ball throughout the pitching process, mimicking a real pitch and allowing them to time their swings and strides perfectly. This helps train them for the actual field instead of stressing them out and forcing them to develop hair-trigger responses since they never know when the ball will be coming, as is the case with some traditional machines.

What Are the Machine's Features?

Situational customizability: The Hack Attack pitching machine offers many amazing features that will allow your team to train for any pitcher in any situation. Far from simply spitting out straight pitches, it can throw right and left handed breaking pitches like curveballs, split fingers, and sliders, as well as fastballs rivaling major league pitchers. Unlike other pitching machines, its easy-turn dials make it an incredibly simple matter to adjust the type of pitch you want.

Durability: The Hack Attack machine is powerful and the wheels are very long lasting. Durability is one of the best parts of the Hack Attack; its practically indestructible steel frame is impervious to rust and can withstand time and weather for a baseball pitching machine you won't have to replace anytime soon.

Portability: You might think the Hack Attack pitching machine is hard to get from place to place-but we've taken care of that by installing a set of wheels that you can flip up and out of the way when the machine needs to stand on its legs, and down to meet the ground when you need to move it around. It's heavy enough to absorb recoil, but light enough to be transported with ease.

Consistency: Don't you hate it when a machine throws different kinds of pitches at variable speeds, even if you didn't change a single setting? The Hack Attack throws exactly the pitch you want, every single time.

Why Should I Buy a Hack Attack?

If you and your team are really serious about baseball or softball, you should do your best to play like the pros-and this is what the pros use. It's the most superior baseball pitching machine currently on the market, and there's no question that with its tough construction, stability, and weather-resistant treatment, it will serve you well for many years to come. You'll always know where the ball is, you'll be able to mimic the throws of just about any pitcher, you can change the settings with a turn of the dial... the Hack Attack is worth every penny!

FACTS ABOUT WEBSITE SECURITY

Have you any idea the thing it really means to have your website hacked? Do you really understand the implications which it represents? The internet offers a great sector with wonderful convenience to both consumers and businesses. However, anytime a website fails to follow the proper security procedures or not working with a top notch website secure system, they are simply vulnerable to hacking. Once your website is hacked, a few pieces of vital information in your server, such as the personal or financial information which is part of your potential customers who shop with you, or documents which your customers store on your own site, are extremely vulnerable to theft. Moreover, nowadays your costumers are well informed as to what it means if a website gets hacked, considering that it can be quite detrimental to any website where it all diminishes its quality and integrity, as its customers lose trust. Moreover, you lose the rankings by the search engines.

Even though there are a few website security companies against hackers out there, most of the solutions come afterward. This means that, most of the services offer to clean the site from malicious software or viruses right after your site has been hacked. The real solution is to safeguard your web site till the hacking occurs, and therefore continuously monitor your web site for every hacking activities so that you may go ahead and take proper action way before any hackers have the ability to make any attempt. Apart from the protection of your website from getting hacked, there are more precautions you will be taking to help protect your site. The most important measures is to always monitor your files as well as your mySQL database, repair and optimize them continually, and also backing them up to your server or to your desktop.

You might also be thinking the fact that your hosting company provides the utmost website security and prevents hackers from installing malware or viruses on your website. Nothing could be further than the simple truth. When your website will be hacked, the first thing your hosting company does is to de-activate your site to secure their own system. It absolutely was your responsibility to safeguard your web site to begin with, now it's your responsibility to clean up your site in order to open it back to the public.

You should also be a lot more careful if you are using free scripts, not to mention WordPress, Joomla or Drupal, as hackers know the weaknesses of the above platforms as your site is getting vulnerable. It is your responsibility to safeguard your website, and there really is a viable strategy to this matter.

A better solution should be given by the professionals who have thorough experience and data about each aspect of web site security. They have to have enough knowledge as to clean your web site from malware and viruses when your website has been hacked. Most of all, they should have in depth knowledge regarding website security prior to being hacked, determining and knowing the weaknesses of the majority of of the commercial applications like WordPress, Joomla. Moreover, they should be able to do extensive tests to cover all possible angles related to how hackers can easily penetrate your website.

IPHONE HACKS AND THREATS TO PERSONAL PRIVACY

We've been amazed by it since its introduction. Who can't remember the address given by Steve Jobs of Apple when he introduced the revolutionary iPhone? Who wasn't amazed at the device that was capable of surfing the web, taking pictures, listening to music and of course receiving and placing calls?

Nothing new, right?

Just as the iPhone was released, hackers around North America started to dig into what makes this tick. The primary reason was to unlock the phone so that you didn't have to sign-up with AT&T but with any carrier that supported the technology. But could there me more nefarious reasons to hack the iPhone?

Skilled hackers could now take their phone onto any carrier, but more importantly they could create and enable custom ring tones (without having to pay for buying ring tones), enable custom wallpapers and more.

In process of hacking into the iPhone, several tidbits were gleaned - such as the fact that the software on the iPhone runs as "root" - in the Unix world this basically gives you full and complete access to the machine. You could bring down entire servers and even chains of servers if you have ROOT access to a Unix machine.

So how does this impact you, the average user of the Apple iPhone that isn't planning on hacking into their phone? Well someone may want to hack into your phone and they now have the blueprint to do it.

While Apple is working hard to try and prevent hacking by playing cat and mouse game, it will always be a cat and mouse game. If you happen to surf into a questionable website that happens to download software to your iPhone you could end up in a whole heap of trouble.

In an article in the New York Times Technology section from July 23, 2007, an iPhone flaw was found to let hackers take over the iPhone. Remember that most people store entire lives on their digital assistants (whether this is a Smart Phone, the iPhone or even a PDA). They keep names, addresses, phone numbers, e-mail addresses on them. Not to mention passwords, banking information (such as bank account numbers) and even digital images taken by the built-in camera.

Now imagine if a hacker has access to all this data.

The security firm, Independent Security Advisors found that through common flaws (and without even hacking into the phone) they were able to gain unauthorized access to the contents of the phone through a WiFi connection or by tricking users into visiting websites that insert malicious code onto the phone.

How can you protect yourself? As with any device, common sense should prevail. Don't open e-mails from people you don't know - if you open them, and there are attachments avoid opening the attachments or visiting the websites in question.

Since the Apple iPhone has automatic updates, always ensure your iPhone has the latest updates by visiting the manufacturer's site.

HOW TO REPAIR HACKED BLOG

Almost everyone with an e-mail ID or even a computer with internet has been hacked into at some point or the other. It is not a good feeling, I know.

It's even worse when your blog or website gets hacked into and someone messes things up. However, there are ways that you can repair your blogs or websites and safeguard them against hackers.

Hackers usually target big companies and homes where using the internet and computer is vital on a day to day basis. Big companies should use a service called Copendium. It is a blogging platform for big corporate institutions and keeps safe the websites and blogs.

Copendium offers a team always monitoring your daily work without busting into your private files. Here, I share with you the steps you can take to repair your hacked blog or website.

First, if you notice that your blog has been hacked, avoid downloading a bunch of software that you think will help. That is our first reaction, but it is wrong. Panicking is not going to solve anything. Just relax and follow these steps.

Second, remove access to the blog as soon as possible. The best way is to assign another name to the index.php file. All scheduled posts to your blog should be stopped immediately. You should send a message to your subscribers saying that you are offline and the blog is under repair. Hackers do everything online and thus, with an open line available, it will make their work easier.

Third, remove all your themes and take a back up of your blog or ask your web host for the backup files. Do not only keep a back up for your files, a back up for your blog is very important when a situation arises that you cannot control. Themes are also an easy way for hackers to get into your system and create a mess for you to clean up.

Fourth, all plugins should be completely removed. Plugins are the simplest way of hacking into a blog by inserting codes into the system.

Fifth, check the database. It is very important to take a look at the database and to see if you can find any security holes or gaps where hackers can find a way in. It is very important to see that all possible ways to enter the blog or website are closed off.

Last, the reinstallation of plugins and themes, is the last and final step to the recovery of your hacked blog. After these steps are complete, run the blog and check if it is working as before. Hopefully it is and now without any threats.

If you cannot do all this yourself, hire a programmer to do it for you. You can find one who will do it for just $5 on fiverr.com. If you were one of the many whose blog was hacked, these few steps should help you repair and recover it.

HOW CAN HOSTING ACCOUNTS BE EASILY HACKED

Hacking of web sites and severs are on rise recently. Hacking is done by some individuals using different methods to achieve their goal. As you know hacking means an unauthorized entry or penetration into another network or computer to gain complete control of its functions. Most of the people using emails now these days are experiencing different kind of hacker attacks either through email or through unauthorized software installation or by plug in equipments. The worst part of it is that nobody will come to know that a program is doing a spying on your activity or somebody else controlling your network.

Most hackers taking advantage of your lack of knowledge about how the latest technology works and what are the latest techniques. For many people, once software is installed, they never bothered about its maintenance such as upgrading the software to have the latest features and omission of errors which occurred in the previous version of the software. Previous versions of software might have come with security lapses and the programmers taking care of it in a later stage and which is available as upgrade patches.

Hacking through email is not new. Hundreds of fraud mails are received in the spam folders every day and many of them with attachments. If you opened an attached file, it will automatically install a software in your computer mail box and from there to the mail server. It will spread rapidly across all the mail accounts and their computers. Hence its always important to first ensure that the website links you are clicking in your email inbox are secured and are not from websites which look fishy.

External hard disks, pen drives, floppy disks, games, attractive backgrounds are all will be coming with some kind of scripts which automatically installed in to your systems. Never upload a file to your server's ftp accounts from a unknown source or external media which is not scanned for virus, malware or spywares.

Use of weak passwords to remember them easily will be resulting in hacking of the system. A password which is difficult to find out contains upper and lower case characters, numbers and signs will be good. Make use of different online tools to generate a secured password which cannot be easily hacked.

Secured network is the need of the hour and regular maintenance and checks should be dome frequently to get rid of hackers, especially when your clients are engaged in ecommerce.

PENALTIES FOR EMAIL HACKING

As innocent as it may seem, hacking into another person's email account is considered a serious offense in the eyes of the law. Depending on the circumstances surrounding the hacking, an offender may be charged with a second or third-degree felony, which generally results in severe penalties.

Hacking is the online equivalent of tampering with another person's mail. Anyone may be charged with hacking, regardless of the offender's relationship to the person whose account was illegally accessed. In fact, most hacking cases involve family members, partners, or spouses accessing an email account without the owner's consent. In all cases, the victim may press charges against the perpetrator, and if he or she is convicted, there will be a felony offense on his or her record.

Felonies are serious offenses that are punished with either jail time, fines, or a combination of both. Generally, hacking is a third-degree felony; however, if the act was committed in order to steal information, defraud, or otherwise harm the victim, the offense may be escalated to second-degree felony. The penalties for these offenses are as follows:

Felony of the Third Degree

Up to 5 years in prison

Up to $5,000 in fines

Felony of the Second Degree

Up to 15 years in prison

Up to $10,000 in fines

In addition to possible jail time and steep fines, a felony conviction can have devastating effects on an individual's professional and social life. With the help of an attorney, however, you may be able to have your charges reduced or dismissed entirely.

HOW TO STOP YOUR HOTMAIL EMAIL ACCOUNT FROM BEING HACKED

Hotmail email accounts are the easiest and most hacked email service provider. You should be aware that your Hotmail email account is easily hacked. Just recently, 10,000 Hotmail email accounts have been hacked, and all 10,000 accounts have been publicly listed online with all the name and passwords of the account. According to Microsoft, the owners of Hotmail, stated that the causes of the email hacks was due to a phishing scheme. Basically what this means is that the name and passwords were stolen through an email that allows it to steal your password. You can prevent your hotmail account from being hacked by following these simple steps:

1. Do not login your Hotmail account in any public computer or internet café. These computers are a haven for hackers, because

they allow programs to run in the background without you knowing to steal your password. Also, most public computers do not have any anti-virus software at all, so viruses have easy access to your computer leaving you in risk to attack.

2. Don't have simple or single word passwords. Passwords that are simple or have passwords less than 11 characters can easily be hacked. This is because they can be brute force hacked by cycling through a large dictionary to get into your email account. So when creating your password, make sure it is at least 11 characters long and mix it up with numbers. For instance, hu87hs65hna. Make sure you remember it!

3. Don't use the same password twice. If they somehow do get your password, all of your other accounts, such as your bank account can be hacked with the same password.

4. Passwords should be ideally changed monthly. If someone somehow gets your account, you can stop them in their tracks straight away when you change monthly.

5. Use anti-virus software such as McAfee or Norton's Security to protect yourself from virus. Some virus can capture your password, so these preventions are a good measure.

6. Don't have passwords visible anywhere on your computer. If you have your account name and password all in one word file, you are susceptible for your password to be stolen. Keep it private!

INCREASING TRAFFIC TO YOUR WEBSITE BY GETTING HACKED

Normally the amount of traffic your website receives is quite uniform. Between one day and the next not too much changes. Growth is slow and steady.

But there might come a day when you see a sudden and large spike in traffic. At first you might be excited thinking that your site has finally took off - that it is finally going to succeed. Maybe, but maybe not.

True, one possibility is that your site was mentioned on a social network or popular blog and that explains the rise in traffic. But there is another more sinister possibility - your site has been hacked.

How to tell that your website has been hacked?

1) Increase in traffic

The first and most obvious clue is a sudden raise in traffic. A hacked site usually means that somebody put webpages on your site and sending traffic to your site to view the pages.

The pages are usually information gathering pages. Hackers place a fake banking update page on your site and send people there to fill it out. Not suspecting fraud, people fill out the banking info and then by clicking submit they send their private banking information to the hackers. The hackers then use the information to access the bank accounts.

Therefore, the increase in traffic you notice are people filling out banking information forms on your website.

2) Increase in page views of pages you did not create.

Check your states. Are there any pages that you did not create that are receiving lots of page views?

Usually the hacker is able to access one of your folders because of incorrect security settings. They places all the banking update pages in the folder. Look for strange page names with lots of page views.

If you find such a page then have a look at it. Download it to your local computer and open it in notepad. Do not run it - it might be a script. Just open it in notepad and try to figure out whether it is something that should be on your website or not.

3) Check referring sites

Go through your referral sites and look for odd sites sending you traffic. For example, a site that has nothing to do with your niche. Or a site that suddenly appeared and is sending you lots of traffic.

Visit the site and search for a link back to your site. If you cannot find a link back to your site then that is a good sign that the hackers are using the site to redirect traffic to your site.

What do if your website has been hacked?

The first thing is contact your web hosting service. Tell them what you have found.

Either they will remove the hack and increase the security of your website or they will recommend what needs to be done.

For most hacks the resolution is to remove the foreign pages, block the suspicious referring sites from accessing your websites, getting the latest updates for any applications and tools used on your website, and checking the permission settings on all the folders in your public folder.

By keeping your website up to date with the latest patches and updates you reduce the chance that a hacker will exploit a security hole and have access to your website.

Having your site hacked does increase your traffic but in almost all cases it is not the kind of traffic you want.

WAYS YOUR CAR COULD GET HACKED

Would you in a million years believe that your car could get hacked? Like the way Zappos, Inc the online mega shoe store, got recently hacked. Their cyber security system could not stop online hackers who in the end gained access to about twenty four million customer's account details and private information. You may be more vulnerable than you think when it comes to securing private information, since cyber vulnerabilities extend far beyond the internet, banks, and social networking sites. It can definitely be applied to your car. Read on to find out the ways in which your car could get hacked.

The researchers took a basic mid-sized car, moderately priced, not too fancy, as a study sample. What they found was that there were many ways to hack into the vehicle, even remotely. But it did not just end there.

Surprisingly, they found that the number of ways to access private information in the vehicle was parallel to the amount of hacking that could be done online, in a more traditional computer sense of the word, "hack".

First off, instead of targeting a single car in particular, these hackers might threaten a large group of cars. By monitoring the location of several most valuable ones that make it sufficing to go through all this risk, hackers are able to sell unlocked cars to robbers and thieves. This means they can secretly track cars using GPS coordinates and VIN numbers and then plan to carjack at their leisure and in terms of demand.

Secondly, once a car has a compromised GPS tracking information, its movements can be easily watched and tracked down. Anything you see in movies may be done, since devices that makes it easy to eavesdrop on in-car conversations are so easy with the advance of portable technology. The hacker could also learn about the car owner's daily lifestyle and exact routines. Even scarier, they will be able to find where the car owner lives.

You may not know this, but hackers can penetrate virtually any phone and access mass amounts of data. This means they can track your car down simply because you have a cell phone in the car. Later they may be able to use the cell phone as a trigger device that disengages the brakes or something even worse. Yes, we're on the same page, something like blow your car up. Although only very professional hackers will be able to do this, it's not entirely too impossible Remote exploitation of cell phone devices.

To be clear, although these fiascos don't happen all too often, the thought is definitely scary because it could happen in the future.

To calm your nerves there are a number of ways you can protect yourself. For example, making sure you have a comprehensive car insurance policy that will insure you against theft, replacing your car, protecting valuables in your car, and other safety measures. Consider installing alarm devices and systems, and get your car checked regularly. Car insurance companies will have to change their policies in the near future to account for these advances in hacking and car theft, but until then you should always compare car insurance rates so you can get the best deal and protect your car with the most comprehensive plan out there.

SOLUTION TO HACKED FACEBOOK OR TWITTER ACCOUNT.

Unfortunately, this scenario is a reality for all of us who use social networking -- it's not a matter of IF your Twitter or Facebook account will be hacked, but simply WHEN. I've been on the receiving end of messages from my friends whose accounts have been hacked. The message typically compliments me on some body part or requests me to click on a link to view a video of myself. Also, there are usually a number of misspellings in the message.

Be very careful when you get those kinds of messages, even when they are coming from trusted friends who would normally not engage in this type of behavior. Many of the messages are linked to a virus or some type of malware that either infects your computer or will gain access to your account and send all of your friends and followers spammy messages. If you do slip and click on one of these links, pay attention to what your virus scanning software tells you, especially if you get a security warning about a site.

If your Twitter account is hacked:

1. Visit Twitter's information page for problem resolution.

2. Log out of Twitter

3. Clear your browser cache (your browsing history and cookies and private info) and close down your browser.

For Internet Explorer: Go to Tools -- Internet Options, and then click on the "Delete" button under Browsing History. Check all of the boxes (except InPrivate

Filtering data) and click on the "Delete" button.

For Firefox: Go to Tools -- Clear Recent History, and then click on the down-arrow next to "Details", check all of the boxes, and select "Everything" for the time range to clear.

4. Open a new browser window, log into Twitter, and change your password. You can also use the Twitter password reset feature to set a new password before logging in again.

5. Visit your settings page and check your Connections. Revoke access for any third-party application that you don't recognize.

6. Submit a support request to let them know you have taken all of the proper steps to reset your account and to request that your

direct messaging capability be restored. You can also include info on any statuses that weren't posted by you in the body of the request.

7. Update your password in all of your third party applications as well. If a third party application (like Facebook, Twitterrific, Twhirl, etc.) is trying to use your old password to access your tweets, it will lock you out of your account.

If your Facebook account is hacked:

1. Visit Facebook's information page for problem resolution.

2. If you are still able to access your login email address, then use the "Forgot your password" link to prompt an email from Facebook with a password reset code. If you

can't access your account, then use the link above.

3. Clear your browser cache (your browsing history and cookies and private info) and close down your browser as described above.

4. Your account could also have been phished/hacked by a phishing web site, worm, or malicious software. To ensure that all is safe again, refer to the "Warnings" section on Facebook.

Take care when using Twitter and Facebook. Trust your intuition, and if something doesn't look or feel right, ignore it or delete it before clicking on it. You will have probably saved yourself hours or headache in trying to restore a hacked account.

SUPERB PRODUCTIVITY HACKS THAT EVERYONE SHOULD TRY

Productivity is something we are all concerned about. It is the ability or state of producing something good for yourself by using your available resources efficiently. Time is the most important resource of us, but being humans we get distracted easily which ultimately leads to procrastination. Procrastination strongly affects our productivity. So, all you need to do is, try to get rid of this bad habit. It's just a mindset that can be changed easily by committing yourself to change it by heart. Therefore, instead of wasting time on irrelevant tasks, use it effectively to boost your productivity.

Here are some superb and easy to do hacks that are equally helpful for all of us, an employee, freelancer, leader or a manager. These productivity hacks are essential to try if you really want to manage your time and need a positive change in your performance. So let's see what are these amazing tips or hacks:

1. Perform Your Biggest and Most Important Tasks of the Day First

Prepare a list of 3-4 most important tasks to do at the beginning of the day. It will not only restrict your procrastination but also help you to stay productive and focused throughout the day. As we feel more energetic in the morning, so it becomes easy to tackle the most difficult tasks. Now come towards easy tasks, you can follow the 2-minute rule for that. The task which can be done in 2 minutes, go for it. Try to finish each and every small piece of work in time instead of setting it aside and making it a big snowball.

2. The Pomodoro Technique to Manage Breaks

It's a special time management technique that enables people to work within their available time rather than looking for it. Now how to use it? Simply divide your whole working day into small periods of time that is 25 minutes having a 5 minutes break. These short periods of time are called "Pomodoros". After passing about 4 Pomodoro, you have to take a bit longer break i.e. 15-20 minutes.

The basic purpose of this method is to create a sense of urgency. So now instead of feeling that you have plenty of time to complete your work and wasting it on irrelevant things, you will focus on your tasks to make more progress. Moreover, it also makes you feel a little lighter as it releases tension during break time and make you breathe well.

3. Set up Mini Tasks

Whenever you have to complete a big project, split it into small tasks and design a checklist. Now start with the easiest one until you complete the whole project. You will feel a little relaxed because the part of work you just have finished, ultimately will give you a sense of accomplishment.

4. Stop Underestimating the Power of Distractions

Wherever you go, distractions follow. While working in your office you may face talks near water coolers, a colleague who's having fun on his desk or even a newspaper at your own table can distract you. So working at home in a peaceful room seems a little dreamy to boost your productivity, isn't it?

NO, this is not true. Actually, these little distractions from your working environment give your mind a little boost in terms of quick breaks and help you get back to your work easily.

But beware! Sometimes distractions trouble a lot. Like keep checking your phone, social media accounts, many gossips during work or something else can divert your attention and moods easily. So be wise, if your distractions are pushing you back from work rather than boosting your productivity, weed them out.

5. Build Friendship with Red and Blue

As per scientific study about "Which colors improve brain performance", red and blue are very significant.

The study reveals that red color is associated with the ability of the mind to pay more attention to details while blue color gives a spark to your creativity.

So add these colors in your pick-list and make friends with them. Try to decorate your workplace area with these two colors because they are beneficial for your brain and pleasant to the eyes as well.

6. Keep asking yourself if whatever you are doing is Productive at all?

Most of us waste a lot of time doing irrelevant things in life or work; like using Facebook, useless conversations at home, taking selfies all the time or making too long phone calls that are not productive or beneficial at all. So keep checking whatever you are doing, it is worth doing or not.

On the other hand, develop a habit of rewarding yourself for completing any task or reaching a goal. There are so many ways to reward yourself for eating your favorite meal or buy your favorite thing etc. It will not only make you happy but also motivate you to be more productive.

7. Bullet Journaling

This is the productivity hack which everyone would love to try especially computer geeks and organizing whiz. It is a new well-designed system to place all of your thoughts in, making yourself disciplined and polish your creativity.

All you need to have is, just a system consisting of notebook or a diary, pencil, erasers, rulers and some colors or highlighters. You can make easy to-do-lists having headings of months, some columns of defined tasks and time to perform them. This will help you to increase your output by analyzing what is done and what is left to be done.

SECRET SOCIAL MEDIA HACKS YOU WANT TO TRY NOW

There are always new and exciting updates on social media sites. And here you will get to know about secret social media hacks you want to try now.

There are a number of secret social media hacks but here we will discuss some of them for Facebook, Instagram, Pinterest, Twitter and LinkedIn.

Instagram

Share Instagram Images Elsewhere After Uploading.

• Share the image to Twitter or Facebook once uploading it to Instagram.

• As we know that you can share the image instantly once you upload it to the Instagram, but you can also go back to any of your images and share an Instagram image.

• First of all, decide which Instagram photo in your gallery you want to share. Go to down in the right corner and click on the ellipsis button and select "Share".

• The images and caption appear where you can edit what you originally posted on Instagram, so you can do any modification to what has been written before you share it. Then select what social media site you want it to post on and then share it. Yes, it's Done!

Take Better Photos without Posting Them

Set your phone to Airplane mode and start taking snaps. It will be saved to your phone but it will not get posted instantly to

Instagram. It helps you to pick up the best image to be posted on the Instagram.

Best Time To Post on Instagram

• Have you ever thought what will be the best time to share that tricked out Instagram images?

• Well, Iconosquare analyzes your post history and interaction on Instagram and tell you the best time to post Instagram photos.

• Moreover, you can also view your most engaged followers, most liked, your new follower and a lot more.

Facebook

• Just customize What You Share on Facebook and with whom.

• Don't want your father to see that photo? Or some post your boss could see? It's quite easy with this simple hack:

• Click on the tab to the left of your post and choose "More Options" and Facebook will pop up another page for you. Just enter the name of people you don't want to share your post or images.

Download Your Facebook Pictures

Pick&Zip app will let you download all your photos and also collect photos you are tagged in. You can also download pictures from Instagram.

Hide from Your Annoying Friends?

You must have that friend who always started chatting once he/she caught you online. Yes, there is a hack for them. Go offline for a specific list of people you don't want to chat often.

Pinterest

How to Pin Something from Facebook

• Just Click on the Facebook picture you want to pin.

• Right-click the image (or control + click on a Mac) and choose "Open Image in new tab" in the drop down menu.

• Then you will be able to pin that picture from that particular page.

Highlight Text Before Clicking "Pin It

When you highlight any text on a page that you want to be pinned and click "Pin it", the text that you highlighted automatically get added to the description box.

Twitter

Download Your Tweet History

• Do you know you can download the tweet history?

• Twitter let you request your archive.

• Twitter gives you the ability to request your archive. You need to go in Twitter Account Setting for your profile; you will get a little option at the bottom of your page, just click on that.

LinkedIn

LinkedIn gives you the option to view other's profile without being known as you had viewed his/her profile.

You just need to follow these steps:

• Just go to "Privacy & Settings" of your profile when you hover over your LinkedIn profile image in the upper right of the page.

• Go to the tab "Privacy Controls", and click on the option for "Select what others see when you've viewed their profile" as the option

• And select the totally anonymous option, you lose a bit of history, but, it's up to you and why you'd want to surf LinkedIn anonymously.

BACKING UP YOUR SITE AND HOW TO REDUCE THE RISK OF BEING HACKED

Pure HTML or PHP Based Websites

The beauty of a Pure HTML website is that it is not hackable. Hackers can only change their own copies of the site and thus cannot hack my website through any HTML weakness since the code is downloaded to the viewers computer. HTML cannot write files to the server nor can it change existing files.

It is possible to turn on PHP functionality for HTML documents at which point the HTML documents become just as vulnerable to attack as a PHP based website.

PHP, if not written correctly can create weakness in the website where a hacker can do incredible damage or only minor damage according to the mindset of the hacker.

Web Site Security

WordPress, Joomla, plugins or components and other PHP Scripts can have weakness that will make it possible to hack a site. When a weakness is discovered the developer of that script will release an update to fix the PHP weakness and then publish a release notices to indicate the threat level or other recommendations about updating to the newest version of their script. This is why it is ALWAYS Recommended to upgrade your scripts as soon as an update becomes available.

As a web-designer often times I find that people run with very old scripts and then wonder why they were attacked, or who would want to hack me, my site is a low traffic site with no importance to anyone. Having old and out-dated scripts on your account is like placing a stack of thousand dollar bills on the table and then leaving it unwatched in an unlocked home with a sign on the front door that says Free Money, come on in.

If you want to reduce the risk of getting hacked then you need to reduce the footprint of where you can get hacked. Uninstall plugins or themes that you are not using. Always Update to the latest version of any script, component, plugin or theme.

Backups

Why would you put so much work into your website and then trust an automatic backup system to hold your site backups. To be wise you should create a backup of your website, data and database and then download that backup for future use.

If you value your content on your website then back it up and back it up often. Just think how much data could be lost if, you do not have a good backup. This will help you to understand how often you should do your own system backup and then you should store that backup offline where it is secure from any hackers or some other unforeseen condition on the server.

Never Trust a Backup

Is it enough to simply backup your data and then put it away thinking all is good? No!

You need to verify the backup if you just download your backup but never check it to make sure it is complete then you may someday be sorely surprised by an incomplete backup. It can happen and does from time to time.

If you download your backups for offline storage and then also test your backups. When the time comes for you to restore that backup you will know that you have something that will work. And that you can restore to get your site back up and running in case something goes wrong.

It may be a good idea to have more than one backup copy. Your own system backups can get corrupted, damaged or lost. I have a backup on my Hard Drive, USB and RW-DVD. You will need to determine the best practices and methods you need to store backups of your websites.

CONCLUSION

Many people would be confused to read about the benefits of ethical hacking. To them, such a concept does not exist as hacking in itself is automatically viewed as unethical or illegal. Indeed, hacking is normally all about the breaching of barriers that have been put in place for the protection and security of the people. So to talk in terms of benefits of such acts is naturally quite alien to people (at least initially.)

Initially hacking really was all about the breaking of laws and accessing information that should not normally be accessed by certain groups of people. But life is never as black and white as we may first perceive. As such, it will come as a surprise to a good number of people that several major computer companies such as IBM, Microsoft, and Apple all have a large and dedicated team of hackers. Yes, you read that right.

They are not, however, breaking any laws so far as anybody can tell. No, these types of hackers are there for entirely good reasons. They are used as security testers for all sorts of programs. Basically, whenever a company comes up with a program, they'll usually bring it to their team of hackers who will then have a go at it ("hack") to see how many holes in security the program has.

They will see if the program can be exploited in anyway and then return it to the programmers along with a list of the vulnerabilities found. This is just one of the benefits of ethical hacking. The program can then be fixed, or strengthened, and sent back again to the hackers to confirm whether there are still any problems with it.

The aforementioned is just one example of the benefits in carrying out hacking. Did you know that there are actually courses being taught on this subject as the demand for hackers has actually increased? As the world becomes ever more reliant on computers, the potential damage that can be caused by a hacker, or groups of hackers, has grown to whole new levels. This is not something large companies can afford to ignore.

As such, learning how to be a hacker can lead to a very promising career indeed, working for one of the many major companies. As discussed, there are several good reasons for ethical hacking to be carried out "in-house" and all of them can help companies potentially save millions of dollars, and minimize the risk of ruining their hard earned reputation with their customers and peers. It is not only the companies who benefit but the people who buy their programs as well.

A team of good hackers can make sure that a program is as safe as possible, making the work of any would-be hacker that many times harder, often forcing them to move on to easier targets. This makes sure that any programs in wide circulation will rarely be tampered with and help protect the privacy and integrity of the computers of people all around the world.

In business, infrastructure equals money. In order to scale, you need a flexible infrastructure to handle the growth. With that said, when centralized infrastructure turns into bureaucracy and slow response, the company becomes lethargic. Hacking work examines these problems from the workers standpoint and outlines things you can do to get your work done by working smart.

Why is this important to me?

I am not doing this summary to waste your time. It is my vision to provide concise action steps that you can adopt right now to reach your entrepreneurial goals. Most companies today trust their vendors and customers more than their employees. This is a real problem because brilliant results require team work and you cannot have a cohesive team if there is no trust. Companies want transparency and centralization similar to command and control systems. This is not a bad thing until it takes a sales man 2 hours to enter an order or if the company blocks Facebook, twitter and LinkedIn. Stupid actions like this kill results.

Results are the name of the game. If you do not get results NOW, you are dead. The hub and spoke model for business is not a bad model just as long as the spokes have autonomy to deliver to the customers and are not tied up by bureaucracy.

Hacking work is broken down into four sections. For the sake of time, I will highlight one point from each section.

1. Engaged Team Members - This one point sums up the whole book and separates great businesses from crappy ones. Engaged team members are four times more productive and profitable than disengaged team members. This statistic if focused on can transform any business.

2. Slaves to Infrastructure - I understand the need for procedures and infrastructure because you cannot scale without it. With that said, I know that larger companies handcuff their employees with ridiculous rules and procedures that ultimately kill the creative spirit. Hacking Work is all about working around these ridiculous rules and procedures. A simple example of this would be locking down file transfer access from one computer to the next. People today can have access to everything outside their work from their phone. Having stupid policies in place to limit creative freedom for the illusion of security is bad policy.

3. Three Types of Hackers - Black Hacks are the ones that steal, cheat and create havoc. These are the people who have given hacking a bad name. This book does not advocate black hacks. Grey Hacks and White Hacks are what are necessary to get the job done in a more efficient manner. These types of hacks are simply clever work around that save an enormous amount of time and allow workers to use their creative freedom for profit and customers loyalty.

4. Clarity - This one is a big deal. Take a look at the stats: one, three of the top five time wasters all relate to communication. Two, information in companies doubles every 550 days. Three, once every three minutes, the average cube dweller accepts an interruption and shifts her focus, consuming 28% of the day. Creating clarity and simple communication and information sharing networks can cure all of this.

Do not go yet; One last thing to do

If you enjoyed this book or found it useful I'd be very grateful if you'd post a short review on it. Your support really does make a difference and I read all the reviews personally so I can get your feedback and make this book even better.

Thanks again for your support!

www.ingramcontent.com/pod-product-compliance
Lightning Source LLC
Chambersburg PA
CBHW060828220526
45466CB00003B/1018